How Should Wives
Treat Their Husbands?

WIVES
BE SUBJECT TO
YOUR HUSBANDS

The Bible's View of the
Family Series

EDWARD D. ANDREWS

How Should Wives Treat Their Husbands?

WIVES BE SUBJECT TO YOUR HUSBANDS

The Bible's View of the Family

Edward D. Andrews

Christian Publishing House

Cambridge, Ohio

Christian Publishing House

Professional Conservative Christian Publishing of the Good News!

CPH Since 2005

Unless otherwise indicated, Scripture quotations are from the Updated American Standard Version of the Holy Scriptures, 2016 edition (UASV).

WIVES BE SUBJECT TO YOUR HUSBANDS: How Should Wives Treat Their Husbands?

Authored by Edward D. Andrews

ISBN-13: **978-1-945757-57-0**

ISBN-10: **1-945757-57-4**

Table of Contents

WIVES 1 Marriage Is a Gift From God

Ecclesiastes 4:12 Updated American Standard Version (UASV)

[12] And though a man might prevail against one who is alone, two will withstand him. A threefold cord is not quickly broken.

It would seem that no expert or anyone who has studied the situation would disagree that the institution of marriage is a dismal failure today. "Over the past several decades, the nature of marriage has changed. Many people are choosing to live their lives with partners without getting legally married, and Americans are increasingly more approving of this option. (Marquart et al., 2012). Unfortunately, people who do marry have roughly a 50 percent chance of staying married. That is equivalent to flipping a coin on your wedding day. Even for couples who stay married, many reports being unsatisfied in their relationships." Sadly, the statistics do not change just because the couple is Christian.

For those who have entered into a marriage, they might ask can they maintain and improve upon their marriage year after year. For those thinking of getting married, can they find true happiness in marriage, will it last? The answers to these questions and others are largely dependent on whether both the husband and the wife correctly understand what the Bible says to husbands and wives, fathers and mothers, and are they applying that biblical counsel in a correct and balanced manner. If we are wholeheartedly trusting in God, not depending on our own understanding, but rather seeking his will in all that we do, he will show us the path to take.' (Pro. 3:5-6) If we do those things, we will remain in God's love.

Should You Get Married?

For some, Marriage is essential for happiness, as God designed man and woman to get married. It is as though something is missing in life if one is lacking their mate. Yet, during this time while God is working out the issues that were raised by Satan in the Garden of Eden and at the beginning of the book of Job, he has encouraged some, who are able to consider remaining single, so as to serve him more fully without any distractions. Jesus spoke of singleness as being a gift. (Matt. 19:11-12) In addition, the apostle Paul spoke of the benefits of singleness. (1 Cor. 7:32-38) However, let it be known that there is no Scriptural basis for any Christian denomination or Christian leader to demand that anyone remain single. In fact, the apostle Paul warned Timothy that "in later times some will fall away from the faith, paying attention to deceitful spirits and doctrines of demons, by means of the hypocrisy of men who speak lies, ... who forbid marriage." (1 Tim. 4:1-3) There are supposed Christian denominations that have forbidden marriage among its priests for centuries. If we feel the calling to serve God more fully and want to forgo marriage during this time, make certain this is you calling and desire. If, not there is true joy and happiness within marriage if we correctly understand and apply the Bible guidance on the matter.

We do not want to cast a shadow over the institution of marriage. Marriage is also a gift from God. (Gen. 2:18) Marriage has advantages and can possibly bring many blessings. For example, the person who is in a good marriage has the best foundation for enjoying life. Children need and deserve a two-parent family that is stable, with Christian parents raising them based on Bible principles, providing love, discipline, and guidance. (Ps 127:3; Eph. 6:1-4) While raising children is the number one reason for marriage, it is not the only reason.

2

Ecclesiastes 4:9-12 Updated American Standard Version (UASV)

⁹ Two are better than one, because they have a good reward for their labor. ¹⁰ For if they fall, one will lift up his fellow. But woe to the one who falls when there is not another¹ to lift him up. ¹¹ Again, if two lie down together, they can keep warm, but how can one keep warm alone? ¹² And though a man might prevail against one who is alone, two will withstand him. A threefold cord is not quickly broken.

The passage can be used for friendship, A Christian not separating himself from the congregation, and yes, Marriage, which is the closest friendship one, can have. The single person does not have the same assistance, comfort, and protection that married couples can share. The twofold cord can be torn but not as easy a single cord. In a marriage, the third fold of that threefold cord is God. The husband, the wife, and God make up the threefold cord. Therefore, three strands woven or braided together would be much more difficult to tear apart. When pleasing God first is the prime concern of both the husband and the wife, the marriage is then like the threefold cord. If God is truly a part of the Marriage, the union will then be very strong.

Moreover, biblically, it is only within a marriage that sexual desires can be satisfied. Within the marriage, the sexual union is biblically viewed as a source of delight or pleasure. (Pro. 5:18) When a young single person reaches the age when sexual desires are very strong, he or she may struggle with their sexual desires. If these desires are not kept under control, it could lead to unclean, sinful conduct. Paul offers us the following counsel to single people, "But if they do not have self-control, let

---

¹ Lit *there is not a second*

them marry; for it is better to marry than to burn with passion."—1 Corinthians 7:9, 36; James 1:15.

Regardless of our reason to marry, we need to be realistic as well. Paul was quite realistic with those who marry "will have tribulation in their flesh." (1 Cor. 7:28) Those who marry will face difficult times and challenges that single people do not face. Here is where we offer biblically sound information to those who choose to marry, as to how they can decrease the challenges and increase the blessings. The best way is to choose your mate wisely.

Choosing a Good Marriage Mate Based on Scripture

The apostle Paul under inspiration gives a vital principle that we need to consider when choosing a marriage mate. "Do not be yoked together with unbelievers." (2 Cor. 6:14) What did Paul mean by 'being yoked together'? Paul was giving us an agricultural example. A yoke is a wooden frame for harnessing two draft animals to whatever they had to pull. If a donkey and an ox are yoked together, it will be two animals of a major difference in size and strength, meaning that both

4

will suffer. That is because there will be great friction and strain because the strong animal will have to make up for the weak animal. This is the same in the marriage of a believer and an unbeliever. In a marriage between a believer and an unbeliever, there will be the same friction and strain because the believer will have to carry most of the burden being the stronger of the two. The believer will want to be faithful to God in all things, and the unbeliever will likely care little about that. They will not have the same priorities in life. The believer will want to focus on Christian meetings, while the unbeliever will be focused on the desires of the flesh. Much pain and suffering will result from this. Paul thus urged Christians to marry "only in the Lord."—1 Corinthians 7:39.

Loneliness can be a bitter storm to survive. The pain of wanting someone to love and seeing others in love can be overwhelming at times. This can move the single Christian to ignore Paul's Holy Spirit advice and decide that being unevenly yoked is better than no marriage at all, so they marry an unbeliever. It always ends up the same way, at first; it seems to have been worth it. Then, as time passes, the fleshly qualities of the unbeliever begin to take a toll. The believer begins to feel just as alone in the marriage because they cannot share the most important thing in life with their mate. Therefore, it is wise to trust God. (Ps 32:8) It is best to remain single until an opportunity come to "marry in the Lord."

Now, we must state the obvious. Not every Christian is a person worthy of marriage just because they claim to be a Christian. When choosing a mate, we need to seek out the spiritually mature. Do they regularly go to the Christian meetings? Do they prepare for those Christian meetings? Do they have spiritual goals? Do they take their walk with God serious? Do they show that they have a deep love for God? Remember, actions speak louder than words. We need to use the principles of

God's Word to guide us to the mate that will compliment us.—Psalm 119:105.

Ways that You Can Prepare for a Successful Marriage

If you are considering marriage, it is best to ask yourself, "Am I truly ready?" The answer to your question does not really hinge how you feel about love, sex, companionship, or raising children. Rather, you have to think through different goals that need to consider when you are a prospective husband or wife.

If you are a young man or even an older man, consider the Proverb, "Prepare your work outside; and get it ready for yourself in the field, afterward, build your house." (Prov. 24:27) What is the meaning here? In those days, "a young Israelite who was ready to start his own family would need to build a house for his bride and get his farm operating. Which is the first priority? Proverbs advises him to do the **outdoor work first**. He should get the **fields** ready because they were his source of income. The **house** was the place that provided personal comfort, but the crops were the means for supporting the farmhouse. In short, produce before you consume. And a young person contemplating marriage should set up a means to support his family before he starts one."[2] Yes, this young man needed to consider, "Am I able to support a wife and any children that may come or are already there?" A man who fails to care for the physical, emotional, mental and spiritual needs of his family is worse than one without faith!—1 Timothy 5:8.

Then, we turn to the woman, who must also consider what her weighty responsibilities might be. God's Word praises the skills and qualities of a wife that

---

[2] Anders, Max. Holman Old Testament Commentary - Proverbs (p. 301). B&H Publishing.

helps her husband, as she cares for the household. (Pro. 31:10-31) If the man and the woman rush into the marriage without considering the responsibilities that lie ahead, they are being selfish and thinking of immediate gratification. By rushing ahead, they are not truly considering what they need to possess in the ways of skills and qualities that add to the marriage. More importantly, they need to consider also how to prepare spiritually.

When we prepare for marriage, we need to consider the roles that God has assigned to the husband and wife. The man needs to recognize fully what it means to be the head of the Christian household. This place within the marriage is not a license to act as an oppressor or some dictator. Rather, he must imitate Jesus Christ as to how he exercises headship over the congregation. Paul said, "For the husband is the head of the wife, as Christ also is the head of the congregation,[3] he himself being the Savior of the body." (Eph. 5:23) "The wife is to be subject to her husband as to the Lord. This does not mean that she submits to her husband in the same way and to the same degree as she does the Lord since the husband might ask her to disobey God. Rather she serves the Lord by having a submissive heart toward her husband and by obeying him as long as it does not require her to disobey the Lord. The reason she is called upon to be subject to her husband is that the husband is the head of the wife, as Christ is the head of the church. As the church is to be subject to Christ, so the wife is to be subject to her husband. This subjection does not mean inferiority. It is clear that male and female are both created in the image of God (Gen. 1:27) and that in Christ, where personal worth is concerned, there is "neither Jew nor Greek, slave nor free, male nor female, for you are all one in Christ Jesus" (Gal. 3:28). However,

---

[3] Gr *ekklesia* ("assembly")

in the overall scheme of things, God has placed all of us in differing positions of authority and submission. The man may be in authority at home but submissive at work. The woman may be in submission at home and in authority at work. The point is, all social order depends on people's willingness to work together and their ability to determine who is the head of certain endeavors. God's intention is that the husband be the head of the relationship with his wife."[4]

If a woman has not matured enough spiritually in the faith, so she can be supportive and submissive when it comes to the authority of an imperfect husband, she should not marry. If a man has not matured enough spiritually in the faith, so he can know that he must always listen to his wife and be able to biblically decide whether her way is the best way or not and that he is not a tyrant over her, he should not marry. In other words, Scriptures have been largely misunderstood and abused by both men and women. The prospective mates must fully and accurately, know what the Bible author meant by the words that he used. Then, they need to ask themselves, "Can I accept this in my heart and apply it in my marriage?"

The marriage mates need to be prepared to care for the special needs of the other. We can apply the Apostle Paul's words to the Philippians, "Everyone should look out not only for his own interests,[5] but also for the interests of others." (Phil. 2:4) "Looking out for our own interests comes naturally. We need, and receive, no instruction for that. We are instructed to look out for **the interests of others**. We are to keep an eye out to discover ways we can help others even when they do not

---

[4] Max Anders, *Galatians-Colossians*, vol. 8, Holman New Testament Commentary (Nashville, TN: Broadman & Holman Publishers, 1999), 173.

[5] Lit not the (things) of themselves each (ones).

see they need such help. The apostle stated in Galatians 6:2: 'Carry each other's burdens, and in this way you will fulfill the law of Christ.'"[6] Paul also wrote, "let each one of you love his wife as himself, and let the wife see that she fears[7] her husband." (Eph. 5:21-33) This fear means the wife should have a deep respect, a fear of displeasing him because of her great love, not a dreadful fear or some feeling of anxiety. Max Anders writes, "In summary, she is to be subject to her husband and to respect him. **Respect** (*phobetai*) literally means "fear." It can refer, however, to the fear a person should have before God, a reverence and respect (Luke 1:50; 18:2; Acts 10:35; 1 Pet. 2:17; Rev. 14:7; 19:5). This type of reverence and regard should characterize the relationship of a wife and her husband."[8]

Therefore, the engagement, then, is not just a time for fun. It is a period where a man and a woman get to know each other. They get to learn how to deal with each other biblically. It is also a time to see if marriage is the best choice at this time, with this person. It is also a time when one needs to be very cautious and have control over themselves. While there is nothing wrong with kissing or holding your prospective marriage mate, it is dangerous to do so when alone. Being physically intimate is natural, a gift from God. However, those who love God more than their future husband or wife, will not put themselves in innocent appearing situations

---

[6] Max Anders, *Galatians-Colossians*, vol. 8, Holman New Testament Commentary (Nashville, TN: Broadman & Holman Publishers, 1999), 225.

[7] to have such awe or respect for a person as to involve a measure of fear—'to fear, to show great reverence for, to show great respect for.'

[8] Max Anders, *Galatians-Colossians*, vol. 8, Holman New Testament Commentary (Nashville, TN: Broadman & Holman Publishers, 1999), 173–174.

because to commit fornication before marriage is no way to begin a lifelong commitment to each other or God. Entering marriage after committing such a serious sin is such a terrible foundation on which you want to build. (1 Thess. 4:6) If you will cheat on God with each other because of sexual desires, does this not indicate that you may cheat on each other for those same sexual desires?

How Can You Make Your Marriage Survive Your Imperfections and Human Weaknesses?

If the marriage is to survive Satan's world, your imperfection, and human weaknesses, both the husband and the wife need to have the right view of commitment. When we read romance novels or watch Hollywood movies, we always find a loving ending, which anyone would crave. However, marriage, in real life, is not a romance novel or movie. In real life, there is no end; it is an ongoing relationship, which goes on for an eternity, and was designed by God. (Gen. 2:24) It is our view of marriage that matters. A common saying is that the couple is "tying the knot." The problem with that saying is it can be viewed two different ways. First, a good knot can be tied to last as long as it is needed. Notice, as long as it is needed. What happens when you decide you no longer need the knot? Second, a knot can be untied.

The popular view of marriage today is that it is only temporary. Many couples enter marriage only thinking of their individual needs at the time. However, the moment the marriage is a challenge, they are ready to end things. NOTE: There are biblical reasons to end a marriage, such as adultery and physical, mental, emotional, and spiritual abuse. Jesus said, "What therefore God has joined together, let not man separate." (Matt 19:6) If we marry, we need to have that kind of commitment, and if it seems like a burden, marriage should not be a consideration. Again, there are reasons for leaving your marriage mate. Thus, we will offer a brief excursion here.

Excursion on Diverse

When Jesus said the only grounds for divorce was/is adultery, the context was his speaking to Jewish men, who were divorcing their wives for insignificant reasons in the extreme, such as cooking a bad meal. In the context and historical setting, Jesus dealt with the issue at hand. The context and historical setting were that Jesus was dealing with a stiff-necked people who were abusing the basis for divorce under the Mosaic Law. Jesus was not dealing with any exceptions to the rule that might come up in life.

However, the Apostle Paul was in a different context and historical setting. Thus, under the influence of Holy Spirit, he offered an exception. Notice how Paul words things,

1 Corinthians 7:12-15 Updated American Standard Version (UASV)

¹² But to the rest I say, not the Lord, that if any brother has a wife who is an unbeliever, and she consents to live with him, he must not divorce her. ¹³ And a woman who has an unbelieving husband, and he consents to live with her, she must not send her husband away. ¹⁴ For the unbelieving husband is sanctified through his wife, and the unbelieving wife is sanctified through her believing husband; for otherwise your children are unclean, but now they are holy. ¹⁵ Yet if the unbelieving one leaves, let him leave; the brother or the sister is not under bondage in such cases, but God has called us in peace.

The first thing to notice is Paul saying, 'I am inspired by God, so I can say this and the Lord (Jesus), did not touch on this, but I am.' Let us take a look at the context and historical setting. Under verse 15 of chapter 7, a husband or wife is not enslaved to a spouse who has left him or her and has refused reconciliation. If the husband or wife, who has been left by the other has done his or her due diligence of trying to reconcile (7:10-13), and they have an unbeliever who will never return, nor ever remarry, the brother or sister is not enslaved and are free to remarry under Paul's words, not Jesus, because Jesus was not dealing with this particular circumstance. Jesus and Paul were not contradicting each other, just as Paul and James did not contradict each other over faith and works. Paul is complimenting Jesus' words because he is dealing with an entirely different context and historical setting. However, if anyone argues that Paul was not offering an exception clause to Jesus' words; then, Paul would be contradicting Jesus. There is no reason for Paul to talk about 'not being enslaved' to their husband or wife if he were not offering an exception clause to Jesus' words about divorce, nor would there be a reason for Paul to say, 'these are not Jesus words, they are mine.' In other words, Jesus did not touch on this circumstance, 'I, an inspired apostle am dealing with it.' Thus, Paul is offering an exception, so there is no contradiction.[9]

Jesus said the only reason for divorce was adultery under the historical context of his discussion with the stiff-necked Jewish leaders. The Apostle Paul was inspired to expand upon divorce based on another context of a spouse who leaves or you separate from because of abuse, who then refuses to reconcile. No one should stay with an abusive person. God did not intend this to be the case. If that person refuses to change; then, the person is refusing to reconcile. The traditional teachings of the church are not what God's Word means in every case any more than the traditional teachings of the Jewish

---

[9] For a longer discussion of this, please go here:

https://christianpublishinghouse.co/2016/10/05/what-is-the-scriptural-basis-for-divorce-and-remarriage-among-christians/

religious leaders of Jesus' day. Jesus said to them, 'because of your traditions, you have made the word of God invalid.' (Mark 7:13) The meaning of a text is what the author meant by the words that they used.

End of Excursion

When you get married, the husband and the wife need to maintain the same biblical view of each other. If each one applies God's word correctly in their lives, seeing the good qualities and efforts of their spouse, the marriage will be a joy. While we are imperfect, we can still have positive views of each other. Husbands and wives need to have a positive view of their mate and make allowance for when they fall short.—Colossians 3:13.

WIVES 2 Surviving the First Year of Marriage

One man admitted a year into the married, "I am so surprised that my wife and I are so different!" "For example, she stays up late at night, and I like to go to bed early" He reluctantly adds, "I cannot understand her moods; they are as confusing as high school math." The thing that got him most was, "I know I was right in the disagreement we just had, but how is it that I am the one always apologizing and feeling bad." Lastly, he says, "She is so critical of how I do household chores. Nothing seems to be good enough."

The wife had some complaints of her own, "My husband barely speaks to me." She goes on, "It is just 'hello,' 'how was your day,' 'thank you,' no real meaningful conversations." She says, "Even when he asks me, how was your day, he does not really mean it because I start to tell him about my day, he moves on to what he wants to tell me." Sadly, she says, "When I am upset and want to talk about it, he starts to listen, but then he interrupts me with what I need to do to fix things. He is more into fixing problems than letting me get the problems off of my chest." She ends with how irritated she is, "Why are men so difficult to understand? How do can we make our marriage succeed?"

If you have just recently gotten married, you likely have faced similar challenges. It is weird how you never noticed these faults and shortcomings that you never noticed when you were dating or engaged. How can you lessen the impact of the "everyday troubles that married people will have"?—1 Corinthians 7:28, Good News Translation (GNT).

First, realize this simple fact. You are newly married, and neither you nor your spouse is an expert on married life. True, maybe both of you had acquired great social skills before you met, even matured as an adult, and they may have served you well while you were dating. Let us face it; everyone puts his or her best foot forward when you are dating. Both work very hard to please the other. The skills and qualities that you and your spouse have acquired in life and throughout the dating process are like the baby steps of life. Marriage will put those skills and qualities to the test, to refine and strengthen them, if you allow that to be the case.

There are two important points here. (1) You need to ponder, consider, meditate on how you can grow and develop the skills and qualities you have. (2) Likely, life requires that you gain new one's skills and qualities. Let us just mention one in passing. From this day forward, practice thinking before you respond. Literally, when your spouse says something to you, stop, pause 3-5 seconds and think about what you are going to say. If you even think, it will hurt or harm, even in the slightest way, do not say it, let go of it. Another, your spouse does not need to know everything all the time. If there is something that happened in your day that will hurt or harm feelings in the slightest way, keep it to yourself. If a woman flirts with you in line at a restaurant and you did not reciprocate to her but instead lifted your hand and said I am happily married. There is no harm or foul here. What purpose does it serve to share that information? It is like when your wife asked you if this dress makes her look fat. You know it does and to top things of it is hideous as well. Truthfully, you can let her know that it is not good in the gentlest way possible without being frank about it.

The best way to improve your skills and qualities is to consult an expert. Once we have the advice from the expert, it is absolutely necessary that we listen to the advice. There is no greater expert than the Creator of man and women, who instituted the first marriage. (Gen. 2:22-24) Here in this book, we will quote many

Scriptures. Many times, we will offer commentary on what the author meant by his words. You will notice how the Bible is able to help you overcome your weaknesses, improve the skills and qualities you have, and acquire new ones that will vastly improve your marriage. The one message that needs to be taken seriously is: apply, apply, and apply.

SKILL – Learn to communicate with each Other

Why is this such a challenge? Because you were used to thinking for one person and now you must realize that your decisions, your comments, and how you act impacts another person, namely, your spouse. When you make a decision, for example, without consulting your spouse, it makes her feel as though she is not involved in the marriage or that her voice does not matter. Worse still, at times you might talk to your friends about a decision and not even consider your spouse's input on the situation.

What is the Solution?

Keep in mind that Jesus said, "are no longer two but one flesh." (Matt. 19:3-6) In the eyes of God, no other human relationship is as important as that between a husband and a wife. If you are going to grow your relationship beyond the first year, good communication is vital.

Much of the historical narrative in the Bible is given to us so that we can learn a lesson from it. If we look at the account between God and Abraham, we see how God communicated with him. See the discussion recorded in Genesis 18:17-33. Notice how God honored Abraham. (1) God explained to Abraham what he intended to do. (2) He listened and allowed Abraham to explain his views on the situation. (3) Even God made a little adaptation based on Abraham's thoughts. You can follow this same pattern by consulting your spouse, listening to

16

your spouse, and accommodating the spouse's concerns to the extent possible

It is best to present your thoughts to your spouse as suggestions, not final decisions or ultimatums when discussing matters that will affect your marriage. Both of you can offer your opinions and evidence that you supports your spouse's insights. You need to show a gentle attitude toward everyone.—Philippians 4:5.

SKILL – Learn to be Sensitive, Thoughtful, and Perceptive

Why is this such a challenge? The world is a melting pot today, and cultures differ. Truly, even communities differ from one another. As you grew up may it was fine to offer your opinion firmly, even bluntly. There are places in Europe that an American ear would consider them to be tactless but it is the norm there to be very direct when expressing themselves. This is something that should be overcome for the sake of the marriage.

What is the solution?

Never assume that your spouse should be spoken to or even likes to be spoken to as you have been accustom to speaking to others. (Philippians 2:3-4) What the Apostle Paul told Timothy should be applied in a marriage as well. "For a slave of the Lord does not need to fight, but needs to be kind to all, qualified to teach, showing restraint when wronged." (2 Tim. 2:24) **Tact** is the ability to avoid giving offense: skill in situations in which other people's feelings have to be considered. **Sensitive** is one who is thoughtful and sympathetic: tactful and sympathetic about the feelings of others. **Perceptiveness** in a marriage is one who is quick to understand: possessing or showing keen insight and understanding. When you find yourself upset with your spouse try to ponder how you would respond to your boss at work or your bosses boss. Would you use the same tone, the same words, or would you choose your words wisely? True, it is sad that you would tone it down out of respect for your boss and fear of displeasing him or her, but you would not do the same for your wife out of respect and love.—Colossians 4:6.

SKILL – Learn to Grow Into Your Role within the Family

Why is this such a challenge? The husband is not used to using his headship that he never had before the marriage. This is a new role you have never had. You have normally just made your decisions without considering others. Maybe you grew up in a family where your father never consulted your mother. Thus, the friction you have been feeling at the beginning of your marriage might be because you are ruling your family like you are the king. The other side of the coin is that your new wife might be demanding of you in things like being tidier around the house. Thus, the two of you could ponder, how does it make you feel when the other is demanding?

What is the solution?

Your Christian husband too might be confusing what the Bible has to say about wifely subjection and what it says about the obedience of a child to his parent. (Col. 3:20; 1 Pet. 3:1) Rather, the Bible says, "a man shall leave his father and mother and be joined to his wife, and the two shall become one flesh." The wife is a compliment (or counterpart) of her husband. God never refers to the child of the house as being a complement or counterpart to the parent. Therefore, it is not honoring your wife when you treat her like a child and demand that she obey you.

Actually, the Word of God urges the husband to treat his wife in the same manner that Jesus Christ treats the Christian congregation. He can make it easier for his

18

wife to respect his headship if he first respects her role within the family. He should not expect his wife straight away and perfectly to express her subjection to him; she is new to her role as well. He is to love you in the same way he loves and cares for himself, even in times of difficulty. (Eph. 5:25-29) If he is doing these things, the wife will, in turn, honor him as the husband and accept him as the God-appointed head. (1 Cor. 11:3) She will recognize that by honoring him, she is also honoring God. She will know that to reject his headship; she will be evidencing how she feels about her husband and God.

When you and your husband are tackling challenging issues that come up, try to focus on the challenge, not each other. Your husband will love you more deeply if you give him some time to adjust to his new role. Moreover, love him more deeply if he gives you the same opportunity. Therefore, buy out the time to discuss how you are going to be patient with each other. However, the moment someone shows a little impatience, this is not the time to say, "You said you were going to be more patient with me." We all are weak, imperfect humans and are bound to fall short many times.–Ephesians 5:33.

Another thing you might try is: do not focus on the way you think your husband needs to change. Rather, you focus in on what you need to do to make changes. If he does the same thing, all will be well. You cannot change another by demanding it, but you can motivate them by making your own needed changes. The husband might be upset by how he has fallen short on exercising his headship; it is recommended that he ask his wife where he might be able to improve. Then, he should apply those suggestions in his dealings with her. You should ask the husband for suggestions on how you might improve as well.

If you and your husband go into marriage thinking that it is going to be nothing but bliss, you are setting yourselves up for failure from the start. You and your husband should expect to make some embarrassing mistakes as you gain experience in the marriage. While you certainly want to take your shortcomings seriously, you have to learn not to take life too seriously. You have to be able to laugh at yourself. Make it your mission to bring joy to your husband throughout the first year of marriage. (Deut. 24:5) Most of all, allow the Word of God to guide your relationship. If God is the focal point of the marriage, the relationship will grow stronger each year.

Study the Word of God together

- You and your husband should have your own personal Bible study that each of you does alone.

- You should have a family study at least two days a week. The husband being the head of the house, he needs to prepare for the studies and make sure it runs smoothly.

- You and your husband need to prepare for all Christian meetings.

- You and your husband need to attend all Christian meetings each week, regularly.

- You and your husband need to have some evangelism program where you are sharing God's Word with others and making disciples.

WIVES 3 Making Christian Marriage a Success

Ephesians 5:33 Updated American Standard Version (UASV)

33 However, let each one of you **love his wife as himself**, and let the wife see that **she fears[10] her husband**.

For the wife, this fear is to have such awe or respect for a person as to involve a measure of fear, to fear, to show great reverence for, to show great respect for the husband. The joy for the groom on the wedding day when he sees his beautiful wife coming down the aisle is limitless. Almost all dating experiences that end in marriage have a similar beginning, in that, the couple's love for each other grew so much that it led to the point of wanting to marry. The vows were that they would remain faithful to each other forever in both good times and bad times. What some are unaware of is, after the wedding, both the husband and the wife will have to make changes if the marriage is to be a success. Our Creator wants us to be happy and enjoy life together as married couples. It will be successful only if it is grounded in his Word. (Pro. 18:22) Even with God's Word, we are still imperfect humans, and we will have "will have tribulation in the flesh." (1 Cor. 7:28) How can married couples lessen those problems? In addition, how can we make Christian marriage a success?

One of the leading qualities in the Bible is love. The thing is, there are different kinds of love that go into a marriage. For instance, the husband and the wife must show tender affection as well as romantic love. The

---

[10] to have such awe or respect for a person as to involve a measure of fear—'to fear, to show great reverence for, to show great respect for.'

apostle Paul tells the husband that he is to **"love his wife as himself**." "This is Paul's third command for the husband to love. While society pressures a man to assert his manhood by snubbing his wife and her wishes, the mature Christian husband does not have to prove anything to anybody. He is free to weigh the needs and wishes of each family member and make decisions in their best interests."[11] It is love based on the principle that creates a marriage, which is truly successful.

Responsibilities of Marriage the Husband and the Wife

The apostle Paul wrote, "Husbands, love your wives, just as Christ also loved the congregation and gave himself up for her." (Eph. 5:25) Husbands, would you die for your wives? "After instructing wives to be subject to their husbands, he instructs husbands to love their wives so completely and so righteously that the wife need never fear or suffer from her life of submission. Husbands are to **love [their] wives just as Christ loved the church**. How did Christ love the church? He **gave himself up for her**. Jesus dedicated his life to the establishment and welfare of the church. He ultimately gave his life for the church. To that degree, and of that quality, the husband is to love his wife. He is to give himself up for her. He is to dedicate his life to the physical, emotional, and spiritual welfare of his wife. Following the example of Christ, he is to give his wife not only all that he has but also all that he is. When a husband loves his wife so completely, the wife need never fear submission."[12] (See John 13:34, 35; 15:12-13)

---

[11] Kenneth L. Boles, *Galatians & Ephesians*, The College Press NIV Commentary (Joplin, MO: College Press, 1993), Eph 5:33.

[12] Max Anders, *Galatians-Colossians*, vol. 8, Holman New Testament Commentary (Nashville, TN: Broadman & Holman Publishers, 1999), 174.

The husband and the wife vowed to love each other through the good and the bad times. What kind of love can help a husband and wife in difficult times? Paul wrote that love "bears all things, believes all things, hopes all things, [and] endures all things. Love never fails." (1 Cor. 13:7-8) "**Love ... always protects.** Major English Bible versions translate the term *protects* (*stego*) very differently from one another. The word can mean "to endure" or "to cover, protect." If Paul had in mind the concept of endurance, he meant that love bears with many offenses and does not stop loving even under the strain of difficulties imposed by others, even going so far as to love enemies (Luke 6:27). If he had in mind the concept of covering, then he may have meant that love will not seek to expose the sins of others. Love handles the sins of others in ways that will not bring exposure or shame. It is evident that Paul limited such endurance or protection. For example, he instructed Timothy that "those who sin are to be rebuked publicly" (1 Tim. 5:20). Likewise, he called public attention to the strife between Euodia and Syntyche (Phil. 4:2). He commanded the Corinthians to stop tolerating the man who had his father's wife (1 Cor. 5:1–13). Wisdom is required to know when and how to protect or to expose, and love always tends to protect. **Love ... always trusts.** Perhaps this characteristic of love is best expressed in contemporary English idiom as: "Love gives the benefit of the doubt." Suspicion and doubt toward others do not indicate affection or love. On the contrary, when someone loves with Christlike love, he entrusts himself to the person he loves time and again. Still, love does not demand that a person trust even when the basis for trust has been destroyed. Love does not give the "benefit" when there is no "doubt." In these circumstances trust is folly. Yet, the general practice of those who love is to trust the good intentions of others as much as possible. **Love ... always hopes.** Loving someone requires maintaining a measure of optimism on that person's behalf. Hope is an attitude that good will eventually come to those who may now be failing. Failure invades every Christian's life, and it often causes others to give up on the one who fails. Yet, Christians who love continue to hope for the best. This optimism encourages others to keep moving forward. This hope is based not on the Christian, but on Christ. The hope of each Christian is that Christ will preserve him to glory. When a brother falls, it is Christ who picks him up and makes him stand (Rom. 14:4). Christ is the one who promised to finish the work he began. Optimism can also become foolishness and wishful thinking. For example, Paul did not believe that the incestuous man at Corinth would repent without undergoing church discipline. **Love ... always perseveres.** Loving someone is easy when the other person does not challenge one's affections by offending or failing. Love's quality becomes evident when it must endure trials. The New Testament encourages Christians to persevere in their Christian walks (1 John 5:2–5). Here Paul had in mind particularly the need to persevere in love for others. Christians should look to the length and perseverance of Christ's love as the standard for their own."[13]

The husband is to be the head of the house, how does he care for this responsibility? Paul wrote, "Wives, be in subjection to your own husbands, as to the Lord. For the husband is the head of the wife ..." (Eph. 5:22-23) What did Paul mean? "While submission 'to one another' introduces this command, it would be a distortion of what Paul said if one were to teach that husbands should submit to their wives just as wives submit to their husbands. There is a general sense, of course, in which a husband must put the wellbeing of his wife or children ahead of his own happiness—this will be thoroughly addressed in vv. 25–33. But this does not

[13] Richard L. Pratt Jr, *I & II Corinthians*, vol. 7, Holman New Testament Commentary (Nashville, TN: Broadman & Holman Publishers, 2000), 232–233.

eliminate the more specific roles in which wives are to submit to husbands, children to parents, and slaves to masters.[14] Having said this, let us qualify the wife's submissive role. (1) It is a position the wife willingly chooses to assume; the husband is nowhere authorized to put his wife in subjection. (2) It is a duty the wife owes because her Lord deserves it, even if her husband does not. (3) It is a limited submission, paralleling the limited submission Christians give to the delegated authority of government (Rom 13:1–2; Acts 4:19–20; 5:29). (4) The word 'obey,' suitable for children (6:1) and slaves (6:5) is not used of wives. [**as to the Lord.**] Christian wives are submissive to their husbands as one aspect of their obedience to Christ. This implies that the wives' ultimate reward comes from the Lord, whether they are adequately appreciated by their husbands or not. [**For the husband is the head of the wife**] The specific basis of the submission of the wife is that God has set the husband in the family as its "head" (κεφαλή, kephalē). Some have argued that this word means only "source,"[15] but the lexical evidence[16] and Paul's own usage in 1:22 are conclusive in support of the meaning "leader" or

---

[14] Andrew T. Lincoln, *Word Biblical Commentary, Volume 42: Ephesians* (Thomas Nelson, 1990), p. 366. It should also be noted that the parallel in Col 3:18ff. does not mention mutual submission; it begins with a straightforward imperative command.[14]

[15] See S. Bedale, "The Meaning of *kephalē* in the Pauline Epistles," *JTS* n.s. 5 (1954) 211–215. More recently, see George Howard, "The Head/Body Metaphors of Ephesians," *NTS* 20 (1974) 350–356; and Berkeley and Alvery Mickelsen, "The 'Head' of the Epistles," *CT* 20 (1981) 264–267.

[16] Wayne Grudem in an exhaustive survey of Greek literature could not find a single instance where *kephalē* has the clear meaning of "source." See his "Does KEPHALE Mean 'Source' or 'Authority Over' in Greek Literature? A Survey of 2,336 Examples," *TrinJ* 6 NS (1985) 38–59. The uses of *kephalē* in ancient literature are consistent with this dictum of Aristotle: "The rule of the household is a monarchy, for every house is under one head" (*Pol.* 1255b).

"ruling authority." In Eph. 1:22 Paul says that God "subjected" (ὑποτάσσω, *hypotassō*) all things under Christ's feet and that Christ was appointed to be "head" (*kephalē*) over all things. Now, in the context of chapter five, Paul clearly intends to use these keywords in the same sense."[17] "In this context the word 'head' has the idea of authority attached to it after the analogy of Christ's headship over the church."[18]

A marriage will be strong if Paul's advice to the Colossians is followed. Both the husband and the wife need to be "putting up with one another and forgiving one another. If anyone should have a complaint against another, forgiving each other; as the Lord has forgiven you, so you also must forgive." (Col. 3:13-14) What did Paul mean? "The idea of putting up with the abuses and offenses of others continues with Paul's call to **bear with each other**. Believers are to go beyond quiet resignation positively to **forgive whatever grievances [they] may have against one another**. Believers have been fully forgiven by Christ (2:13–14), and the forgiven are obligated to become forgivers. The standard for this forgiveness is Christ himself. Paul saves the most important item of clothing for last. Without love, all the other virtues may amount to mere moralism and little else (a thought found also in 1 Cor. 13:1–3). When love is present, there is harmony and unity in the community. It is not clear whether **love** binds the virtues together, completing a lovely garment of Christlike character, or whether **love** binds the members of the community

---

[17] Kenneth L. Boles, *Galatians & Ephesians*, The College Press NIV Commentary (Joplin, MO: College Press, 1993), Eph 5:22–23.

[18] F. F. Bruce, The New International Commentary on the New Testament: The Epistles to the Colossians, to Philemon and to the Ephesians (Eerdmans, 1984), p. 384.

together in mature oneness. Perhaps the ambiguity is intentional. Both ideas make good sense."[19]

Imperfection means that both the husband and the wife will make mistakes. This love is shown in that they marriage mates do "not keep a record of wrong." (1 Cor. 13:4-5) Disagreements are bound to happen more than we might like to admit because the husband and wife were raised in different social settings, different teachers, different friends, different parents, and so on. When these arise, it is best to follow Paul's counsel. "Be angry, and yet do not sin;[20] **do not let the sun go down on your anger,** [27] nor give place[21] to the devil." (Eph. 4:26-27) Both should be eager to say, "I am deeply sorry for hurting you."

Tenderness in Your Marriage

What guidance does the Bible give us regarding sexual relations in marriage? Why do marriage mates need to show tenderness? The Creator offers marriage mates great advice, so as to have a proper understanding of sex in their marriage. (See 1 Cor. 7:3-5.) Both the husband and the wife need to consider the feelings and needs of each other. If a husband is not tender, loving and affectionate with his wife, she may not truly enjoy their sexual relationship. He might fill her physical need to a degree but not her emotional needs. The apostle Peter wrote, "Husbands, live with your wives in an understanding way ..." (1 Pet. 3:7) In other words, sexual

---

[19] Max Anders, *Galatians-Colossians*, vol. 8, Holman New Testament Commentary (Nashville, TN: Broadman & Holman Publishers, 1999), 331.

[20] A reference to Ps 4:4

[21] Or *an opportunity* to the devil

relations in a marriage should never be forced, demanded or coerced. It should never be used as a tool for punishing one's spouse. Rather sexual relations should come naturally. The moments of sex within the marriage should be the right time for both the husband and the wife.

How are we to understand Peter's words that "husbands, [should] live with your wives in an understanding way"? "Husbands should be **considerate** as they relate to their wives. This word (*gnosin*) carries the meaning of "wisdom and understanding." Husbands should approach their marriage relationship intelligently. They are to live with their wives according to knowledge, not fantasy. Marriage is a real-life relationship, not a soap-opera drama. To live with your wife and demonstrate wisdom suggests a deep desire to understand your wife, to get to know her at more than just a surface level. It suggests a sensitivity to her needs and a desire to respond to these needs knowledgeably. In many ways, this sounds like submission, although the language is different. It hints at the concept of mutual submission (see Eph. 5:21). Beyond this, husbands are to **treat** their wives **with respect.** "Treat" has a special significance. Classical Greek writers always used it in reference to what is due from one person to another. The giving of respect or honor to your wife is not simply a "nice guy" kind of thing to do. It is the husband's recognition of her because it is her due. This emphasis is reiterated in the word *respect.* This word is sometimes translated as 'price' or 'precious.' It indicates value and esteem. It suggests the giving of respect because a wife is precious to her husband."[22]

---

[22] David Walls and Max Anders, *I & II Peter, I, II & III John, Jude*, vol. 11, Holman New Testament Commentary (Nashville, TN: Broadman & Holman Publishers, 1999), 50.

Song of Solomon 1:2; 2:6 Updated American Standard Version (UASV)

² May he kiss me with the kisses of his mouth!
For your love is better than wine;

⁶ His left hand is under my head,
   and his right hand embraces me!

Husbands and wives should be tender with each other in sexual relations. Both need to consider the needs of the other first. If the husband is tenderly and passionately try to fill the needs of the wife before himself and the wife is tenderly and passionately try to fill the needs of the husband, it will be the best experience. "**1:1** Marriage is the context in which physical passion and pleasure is set free. The kiss is a universal expression of desire and affection, and the woman (she is called Shulammite in 6:13) expresses her desire for her lover to kiss her and to kiss her deeply and repeatedly. The senses of touch and taste both came together, and the resulting passion was more than she could handle. She said, Your love is more delightful than wine. By describing his romantic, affectionate kisses in this way, she was saying; I find the touch of your lips and the embrace of your mouth sweet, powerful, intoxicating. It sweeps me off my feet. It sets my head spinning. The passionate kiss, we have discovered, is a sign of a healthy, romantic marriage, even more than sex. "The passionate kiss (average length one minute) reveals a lot about your relationship. Considered even more intimate than sex, passionate smooching is one of the first things to go when spouses aren't getting along" (Marriage Partnership, 10). **2:6** In the passion of their love, Shulammite had not lost sight or sense of the warmth, intimacy, and security of their relationship. With one hand he cradled her head. With the other he held and caressed her. It is interesting that the word embrace is used in the Old Testament "both of a friendly greeting (Gen. 48:10) and of sexual union (Prov. 5:20)" (Carr, 93). He was her friend and her lover. Both were important to her. Both are important to all women. No man should forget this."[23]

When our love for God is greater than the love of self, we will not allow anyone to threaten our marriage. Some have allowed their eye to wander in looking at things they ought not. Jesus said, "Everyone who looks at a woman with lust for her has already committed adultery with her in his heart." (Matt. 5:27-28) The Greek behind "lust," ἐπιθυμία [epithumia] is a strong desire to have what belongs to another, as well as becoming involved in anything that is morally wrong, i.e., coveting, lusting, evil desires, and the like. We need to continue to develop and grow our love for both God and our spouse. We would never dream of cheating on God, nor should we ever look at another woman with lust or passion. We must keep in mind God knows every thought we have, even if our wife does not. Moreover, we have to live with our own internal guilt and shame as we hide secret sexual lusting. We need to strengthen our desire to be loyal to both God and our marriage mate.

Problem In the Marriage

Marriage will not be the fantasy that we may have had when growing up. Marriage involves two grown adults dealing with each other's weaknesses and raising children in the Christian faith while trying to cope with Satan's world. These problems within marriage have caused the divorce rate among Christians to be just as high as the unbelievers. Again, the Bible makes allowances for a divorce in the case of adultery and even if a mate is abusive and will not reconcile and repent. God never intended anyone of his servants to live a life

---

[23] Moore, David; Anders, Max; Akin, Daniel. Holman Old Testament Commentary Volume 14 - Ecclesiastes, Song of Songs (p. 145, 184). B&H Publishing. Kindle Edition.

with an abusive spouse. For more on this see What is the Scriptural Basis for Divorce and Remarriage Among Christians?[24] What are some reason for separation and possibly divorce? You, the husband willfully refuses to support your family financially, so much so, that they go without money and food. The spouse is abusing the other physically, mentally, and emotionally without any true repentance.[25] Another biblical ground for separation and possible divorce is when one spouse makes it impossible for the other to serve God, endangering his or her spiritual life.

It is the biggest shocker and test of marriage when a Christian couple comes to realize that marriage is not what they had dreamed it would be and they now are very disappointed, even angry. They had this blissful picture of some romantic comedy television show, or some Nicholas Spark novel. Do not get me wrong, it can be those things, but it is not always, every day those kinds of things. There is much work, pain, and even heartache in all marriages. **In the movies**, the couple wakes up in bed together, looking just as good as when

---

[24]   https://christianpublishinghouse.co/2016/10/05/what-is-the-scriptural-basis-for-divorce-and-remarriage-among-christians/

[25] **Repentance:** The (Gr. *metanoeo* and *metamelomai*) means to repent, to change one's way, repentance. It means that we change our mind as to our sinful action or conduct, being dissatisfied with that personality trait. We feel regret, contrition, or compunction, for what we have done or failed to do. We change our way of life because we have changed our view, our way of thinking, our mindset, our attitude, our disposition with regard to out sinful behavior. We have a change of heart and mind, abandoning our former way of thinking, feeling and acting. The result is our becoming a new self, with new behavior, and having a genuine regret over our former ways. No one can testify but our own spirit that we have repented; we may make professions of repentance, and the world may believe we are thoroughly sincere, but our own spirit may tell us that our profession is false. In other words, genuine repentance will bring about results that we know to be true.– Matt. 3:2; 12:41; Mark 1:15; Lu 10:13; 15:10; 17:3; Ac 2:38; 3:19; 17:30; 2 Cor. 12:21; Rev. 2:5-3:19.

they went to bed. They roll over and passionately kiss each other, which leads to this heavenly sexual experience. **In real life**, the next morning after the first honeymoon night, the couple wakes up next to bad breath, disheveled hair, and nothing like in the movies. Welcome to marriage. Often, the problems initially arise because the couples were brought up in two different settings and they react emotionally different from one another. He sees the in-laws in one like, she sees the money completely different (some stereotyping here), they disagree on how to raise the children or even if they are to have children. The good news is they have the good news of God's Word to guide them.

The Priority In Your Marriage

Our priority in marriage is our love of God followed by our love for our spouse. While we do not neglect our spouses for the love of God, both husband and wife need to give the worship of God priority. (Matt. 6:33) We need to accept the guidance found in the inspired, fully inerrant, authoritative Word of God. (Ps. 119:105) This means that we need to make Christian meeting attendance a priority. (Heb. 10:24-25) We need to have a personal study of God's Word. (Ps. 119:97) The husband and wife also need to study God's Word together. (Eph. 5:25-26) Both need to prepare for Christian meetings, where they know what is being studied that day. (Heb. 5:11-14) Moreover, as a family and individually, we need to share God's Word with others.—Matthew 24:14; 28:19-20; Ac 1:8.

WIVES 4 Let Marriage Be Honorable

Hebrews 13:4 Updated American Standard Version (UASV)

⁴ Let marriage be honorable among all, and let the marriage bed be without defilement, for God will judge sexually immoral people[26] and adulterers.

While this information is predominately meant for the husband, the principles within this chapter certainly apply to women, and needed to be heeded as well.

> If you're under the impression that it's mostly men who cheat on their wives, then you are mistaken. According to new research, many married women are seeking affairs for romance and sexual satisfaction without any plans of divorcing their partner.[27]

On this verse, Thomas D. Lea writes, "**13:4.** Both Jewish and pagan marriages in the New Testament period were characterized by laxity and immorality. Christians have a different approach to marriage. Purity, contentment, and a trust in God are ingredients needed for developing strong Christian families. Two pro-marriage ideas appear in this verse. First, marriage is to be honored by all. Even among believers today the stability of marriage faces strong challenges. Christians must honor marriage as divine in its origin and as right

---

[26] **Sexual Immorality**: (Heb. *zanah*; Gr. *porneia*) A general term for immoral sexual acts of any kind: such as adultery, prostitution, sexual relations between people not married to each other, homosexuality, and bestiality.–Num. 25:1; Deut. 22:21; Matt. 5:32; 1 Cor. 5:1

[27] Why Happily Married Women Are Cheating | HuffPost (July 29, 2017) http://tiny.cc/vb5qmy

and good in its practice. This verse helps us to see that celibacy is not superior to marriage. Second, those who are married must maintain moral purity. The fact that God will judge sexual promiscuity provides motivation for a holy lifestyle among believers. Violators of this command may be celebrated by some human beings, but they will reap eternal divine displeasure (Eph. 5:6).[28]

Taking a deeper look, Bible scholar David L. Allen writes, "**13:4** With v. 4 the subject shifts to marriage and sexual purity. The main clause of v. 4 is both compound and verbless. The KJV supplies an indicative verb in the first clause and leaves it implied in the second: "Marriage is honorable in all, and the bed undefiled." However, most commentators and translators take the author's meaning to express an imperatival idea for three reasons: the following reason clause supports it; the beginning of v. 5 is a parallel verbless construction, but one which indicates the necessity of understanding an implied imperative verb; and the fronted position of the adjective translated "honored" in the clause supports the imperatival sense as well. This verse serves as a specific example of showing brotherly love (v. 1) in that, as Bruce well says, "Chastity is not opposed to charity, but is part of it." Here the author places a high priority on the sanctity and inviolability of the marriage bond. The New Testament affirms the Old Testament's revelation concerning the divine origination of marriage.[608] The first statement, "Marriage should be honored by all," places special focus on the word translated "honored" by its fronted position in the clause. The word itself means to highly esteem and respect. This general statement about honoring marriage is followed by a more narrowed focus on the sanctity of the sexual relationship in marriage: "and the marriage bed[610] kept pure." This phrase refers to

[28] Thomas D. Lea, *Hebrews, James*, vol. 10, Holman New Testament Commentary (Nashville, TN: Broadman & Holman Publishers, 1999), 237.

sexual intercourse within marriage, meaning husbands and wives should remain sexually faithful to one another and their marriage vows. The Greek adjective translated "pure" conveys the meaning "undefiled," "unpolluted," "untainted." It is in the emphatic position in its clause. One implication of this verse is that marriage should in no way be considered as spiritually inferior to celibacy.[612] In fact, Paul warns the church about those who "forbid people to marry" in 1 Tim 4:3. The "by all" construes the dative prepositional phrase in Greek to encode agency: "by all people." Bruce and Hughes likewise take it in reference to people, but view the phrase in a locative sense: "among all people." Others take the reference to be aspectual or circumstantial with the meaning "in every respect" or "in every circumstance." The compound clause is followed by a subordinating clause, introduced by *gar* "for" expressing the grounds of the preceding exhortation: "for fornicators and adulterers God will judge." The term *pornos* in Greek does have a general meaning of a sexually immoral person and can refer to those who commit sexual sins in general, homosexual or heterosexual, outside of marriage. However, used in conjunction with *moichos*, "adulterer," *pornos* is probably best translated in its more restricted sense of "fornication," with reference to anyone who violates another's marriage by engaging in sexual relations with either partner in that marriage. The term *moichos*, "adulterer," refers to anyone who violates his or her own marriage vows by having sexual relations with someone other than their own spouse. The two nouns are used together by Paul in 1 Cor 6:9. Such sexual immorality God will judge, where *theos*, "God," is emphasized in the Greek text by being placed clause final."[29]

---

[29] David L. Allen, *Hebrews*, The New American Commentary (Nashville, TN: B & H Publishing Group, 2010), 608–610.

The Pitfalls of Immorality

Office affairs or affairs between co-workers are the most common place for infidelity to flourish, as the other spouse is not present, while you spend 40-60 hours a week with another. There is more time spent with your co-worker than with your spouse, children, and friends combined! There are far too many reasons as to why this is fertile ground for immorality. The man is getting excessive attention from the woman, who seems to have so much in common, and understands him better than his own wife. Of course, if he would recall, this was the same with his wife some twenty years earlier, as it is predictable of all new relationships. On the other hand, the woman at the office is getting the attention that her husband never gives her at home, and it feels good to be listened to for once. Obviously, if she only realized that if these two were together long enough to get married, he would likely be just as bad as the husband was.

The world that we currently live in is very vile, and sexual morality is no longer a quality that is valued. Please forgive my boldness here, but to help the older ones reading this to understand, I must make a comparison that may seem too much. In the 1950's after a football game, you might find two teenagers kissing in the backseat of a car. Then, that was viewed as loose conduct. However, today, in 2013, teenagers see oral sex as the exact same thing as kissing. To them, it is no different, so after a football game, you might find two teenagers carrying out oral sex in the backseat of a car. The teens today do not find that as loose conduct either. This is the next generation of adults.

What can Christians do to stay safe in such an influential world that caters to the fallen flesh? We might have thought that a book, like Proverbs that is 3,000 years old would be out of date on such modern issues, but God's Word is ever applicable. King Solomon in

Proverbs chapter 5 will give us the answers we need. However, it is up to us to follow the counsel.

Avoid Seduction

Proverbs 5:1 Updated American Standard Version (UASV)

5 My son, be attentive to my wisdom;
   incline your ear to my understanding,

Like many of the other chapters in the book of Proverbs, it begins with the plea for the son to heed his father's wisdom. Immorality is likely the greatest pitfall for any young man. Thus, Solomon takes this issue on five times in the first third of Proverbs. (2:16-22; 5:3-23; 6:24-35; 7:5-27; 9:13-18) If the young man or woman for that matter is to avoid falling into immorality, he or she will need to pay attention to wisdom, the ability to apply Bible knowledge, and listen to understanding, the ability to see into a given situation, so as to ascertain right from wrong.

Proverbs 5:2 Updated American Standard Version (UASV)

2 that you may keep discretion,
   and your lips may guard knowledge.

In order to possess the good sense or the good judgment and sensibility needed to avoid what we will label as innocent appearing situations, that seems innocent enough but is really a dangerous situation that can lead to ultimate downfall. The young one needs to see where there may not even be evidence that there is seduction in the air.

An older woman may use cunning, smoothness, and crafty ways to slip into the affections of an inexperienced young man in the ways of the world. Being innocent, the young man may not perceive her charms. Once he is seduced, he may still find it difficult how he fell into the disgraceful situation that brought about this ultimate wrongdoing. Many young men have lost themselves to the seductive woman, sexually exploited.

Proverbs 5:3 Updated American Standard Version (UASV)

³ For the lips of a forbidden woman drip honey, and smoother than oil is her mouth,

Her **lips**, the contributing factor to the young man's downfall, were used as a figure of speech, in reference to her words. The Hebrew word *zarah* rendered "**stranger**" here in this context was a reference to a woman that had left the Law, who is now a prostitute or an immoral woman. In this Proverb, like is true of most seductresses throughout history, it is not her physical beauty alone, but primarily the sound of her voice and her words that lead the young man astray. **Honey** is the sweetest substance in the ancient Israelite home and is compared to her words. Verse 3 uses the sweetness of honey to illuminate the enticement to sexual immorality that the "strange woman" will wield by her entreaty to a young man with her seduction of flattering and smooth words, **smoother** than oil.

Proverbs 5:4-5 Updated American Standard Version (UASV)

⁴ but in the end she is bitter as wormwood,
    sharp as a two-edged sword.
⁵ Her feet go down to death;
    her steps take hold of Sheol;

What initially seemed so sweet and appealing will only end as bitter as **wormwood**, a leafy plant that yields a bitter-tasting extract. This encounter has the possibility of making one ill, in severe pain, and even leading to death like a **two-edged sword**. That one sexual encounter can lead to death might seem highly unlikely, until the age of seeing the world through the internet. Sexually transmitted diseases, such as AIDS, Syphilis if not treated can cause **death**, certain types of HPV[30] can cause cervical cancer, which if not caught can end in death, Gonorrhea and Chlamydia can cause sterility if not treated; in addition, it can lead to PID[31] which again, if untreated can cause death. Hepatitis B can lead to a debilitating disease and over time failure of the liver. This is all in the age of extraordinary science. Can we imagine in the Ancient Near East, with no medication to treat diseases? Then, death can also come from a spouse that is betray and acts out in rage to take the life of the two violated the marriage bed.

The seductress's steps lead to **Sheol**, which is a transliteration of a Hebrew word that refers to the grave of humankind. The wisdom here would be in taking a moment, to think of the outcome of one's actions, as opposed to the momentary pleasure of immediate gratification.

A distressed inner-self, an unexpected child, a disease transmitted through a sexual encounter, or the breakup of a home, all bitter results of an immoral indiscretion. In addition, let us consider the massive emotionally distraught spouse, who may never be able to trust you again because of your unfaithfulness. It only takes one act of betrayal to alter the course of multiple lives.

Proverbs 5:6 Updated American Standard Version (UASV)

[6] she does not ponder the path of life;
her ways wander, and she does not know it.

Unlike wisdom, the strange woman does not examine or weigh, pay attention or scrutinize, the **path** that she is on, **wondering** through a life of immorality,

---

[30] Human Papilloma Virus

[31] Pelvic Inflammatory Disease

not even **knowing** the end consequences. In other words, through complete ignorance, she has sidestepped the path of life. Does this sound like the person we should allow to seduce us? Her ignorance is a willful rejection of wisdom, and so we should not be deceived by feeling sorry for her. She is the predator, not the prey. Her entire objective is to lure her prey off the path of life.

Do Not Commit Adultery Against Wisdom

Proverbs 5:7-8 Updated American Standard Version (UASV)

[7] And now, O sons, listen to me,
   and do not depart from the words of my mouth.
[8] Keep your way far from her,
   and do not go near the door of her house,

After a section of giving his sons counsel about their unrealistic nature of ideas or desires about the strange woman's suggestion of underlying passion and sensuality, the father enters into another plea for his sons to listen, never departing from his words.

Passing by the door of her house may seem innocent enough, but is really a dangerous situation that can lead to ultimate downfall. The sons need to see where there may not even be evidence that there is seduction in the air. Verse 8 has it contrasted as to the sons warning to keep themselves far from her and do not go near.

The sons need to stay as far away as possible from the door of temptation, the fleshly influence of the strange woman. There is no reason to take the risk of listening to her raspy voice, seeing her sensual figure, exposing them to her immodest clothing. How foolish to place human senses, seeing, hearing, and smell, in the presence temptation.

Proverbs 5:9-10 Updated American Standard Version (UASV)

⁹ lest you give your honor to others
  and your years to the merciless,
¹⁰ lest strangers take their fill of your strength,
  and your labors go to the house of a foreigner,

Is there not a lack of honor on the part of the young man, who gives his body, mind, and heart in the prime of his life, to one who is merely using him for her pleasures? Is it not shameful to seek out immediate gratification, or the selfish passions of another?

The blindness of his passion will cause him not to see the losses he is about to suffer because of following his physical desire. He will lose his **strength** (honor, physical health, sexual vitality, and self-worth). He will lose his **years** (early death or spent unwisely). He will lose his **labors** (cost of adulteress). Bible scholar Longman states, "The point of these verses is clear: The price of infidelity may be high, for everything one has worked for—position, power, prosperity—can be lost either through the avaricious demands of the woman or the outcry for restitution by the community."[32]

Proverbs 5:11 Updated American Standard Version (UASV)

¹¹ and you groan at your end,
  when your flesh and body are consumed,

You were in such a rush to feed your fleshly desires, and now you groan over the pain and suffering that has resulted, such as sexually transmitted diseases. **At your end**, does not necessarily mean the end of your life, but rather the end of the affair with the strange woman.

---

[32] Longman III., Tremper; Garland, David E.; Ross, Alan P., vol. 6, Proverbs - Isaiah, The Expositors Bible Commentary, Rev. Ed., 78 (Grand Rapids: Zondervan, 2008).

Proverbs 5:12-13 Updated American Standard Version (UASV)

¹² and you say, "How I hated discipline,
  and my heart despised reproof!
¹³ I did not listen to the voice of my teachers
  or incline my ear to my instructors.

Regret is all you have left, so you start in with the "only If" or "why did I not." You ask yourself, why did I reject corrective counsel? Why did I not listen to my teachers? Why did I not take instructors words seriously? Why did I allow the strange woman to have her way with me? Why have I ruined my life? It is all too little too late, as I have failed to heed my father's voice.

Proverbs 5:14 Updated American Standard Version (UASV)

¹⁴ I am at the brink of utter ruin
  in the assembled congregation."

Immorality or sexual misconduct can seem like the greatest thing in the beginning until it becomes public knowledge. The family, the community, and the congregation now know, and your shame is unbearable, you are in utter ruin!

Enjoy Marriage

Proverbs 5:15 Updated American Standard Version (UASV)

¹⁵ Drink water from your own cistern,
  flowing water from your own well.

The Bible is not squeamish about sexual relations, and we do well to follow that example if we are to help, our young ones avoid the pitfalls of this world. The cistern[33] or well is poetic expressions for the wife, who satisfies the desires of the husband. This is considered a private water source. Having sexual pleasure with one's wife is compared to drinking refreshing water. This comparison may not resonate with many in our modern world, but ancient Palestine had a dry climate that left them waterless at times. Moreover, they had to dig wells to seek out water, so it was a very precious staple of life.

Proverbs 5:16 Updated American Standard Version (UASV)

¹⁶ Should your springs be scattered abroad,
　　streams of water in the streets?

Just as the "cistern" of verse 15 stood for the wife's sexual affections for her husband, the "springs" and "streams of water" of verse 16 is a reference to the husband's sexual affections for his wife. In other words, verse 16a would read something like, 'shall your [the husband's] springs [sexual affections] be scattered outward [someone other than his wife]? Verse 16b would read, 'in the streets [where prostitutes are], shall there be streams of water [the husband's sexual affections]?' Verse 15-16 gives the reader an analogy that the "cistern" [the wife] satisfies the sexual desires of the husband, and the "springs" and "streams of water" [the husband] satisfies the desires of the wife.

Proverbs 5:17 Updated American Standard Version (UASV)

¹⁷ Let them be for you alone,
　　and not for strangers with you.

May the sexual desires that the husband receives from his wife, be his alone, never to be shared with another.

---

[33] A cistern is an underground tank for storing rainwater.

Proverbs 5:18 Updated American Standard Version (UASV)

¹⁸ Let your fountain be blessed,
    and rejoice in the wife of your youth,

May the husband's sexual desires continue to be quenched by the wife of his youth, not in seeking out a second wife, a mistress, or a prostitute? "Marital love is pictured as enjoying a fountain in Song of Songs 4:12, 15, and this verse develops the same concept. God will bless physical intimacy between a husband and the wife of your youth but not in any other relationship."³⁴

Proverbs 5:19-20 Updated American Standard Version (UASV)

¹⁹ a loving doe, a graceful mountain goat.
Let her breasts satisfy you at all times;
    be intoxicated always in her love.
²⁰ Why should you be intoxicated, my son, with a strange woman
    and embrace the bosom of a foreigner?

To the husband, who has allowed his passions for his wife to continue over the years, she is as desirable and attractive as a female deer, and he is intoxicated with the pleasure she continually brings him, with her body and her love. The husband should reciprocate this to her and her alone. The Hebrew word *shaga*, which is rendered "intoxicated," is generally used in reference sin that is committed unintentionally, like our innocent appearing situation that we have spoken about throughout Proverbs chapter five. On reference work reads,

The primary emphasis in the root [shaga] is on sin done inadvertently. This is indicated in several ways.

_____

³⁴ Anders, Max. Holman Old Testament Commentary - Proverbs (p. 50). B&H Publishing. Kindle Edition.

First, the two derivatives from [*saga, shegia,* and *misgeh*] indicate an act perpetrated in ignorance, not willfully. Second, in the … The Scripture pinpoints at least three causes for such wandering. The first is wine and strong drink (Isa 28:7; Pro. 20:1). The second is the seductive strange woman (Pro. 5:20, 23) versus the love of one's wife, which ought to "captivate" one (Pro 5:19). The third is the inability to reject evil instruction (Pro 19:27).[35]

How do we close out this section, by looking at the implications of our day? Why would there be a need for any man or woman for that matter to place themselves in innocent appearing situations by flirting in the workplace because the spouse it not there, by a teenager living a different lifestyle while at school, or by spending time alone with someone of the opposite sex? Why be enticed into sexual affection outside of the marriage?

James 1:14-15 Updated American Standard Version (UASV)

¹⁴ But each one is tempted when he is carried away and enticed by his own desire.[36] ¹⁵ Then the desire when it has conceived gives birth to sin, and sin when it is fully grown brings forth death.

Proverbs 5:21 Updated American Standard Version (UASV)

²¹ For a man's ways are before the eyes of Jehovah, and he examines all his paths.

We began Proverbs chapter 5, by looking at the consequences of immoral behavior. The reality is that our actions, even our desires that are not immediately

---

[35] Victor P. Hamilton, "2325 שָׁגָה", in Theological Wordbook of the Old Testament, ed. R. Laird Harris, Gleason L. Archer, Jr. and Bruce K. Waltke, electronic ed., 904 (Chicago: Moody Press, 1999).

[36] Or "own *lust*"

dismissed, are "before the eyes of Jehovah." Regardless of how well we might believe that we are hiding inappropriate sexual desires, or worse still acting on those inappropriate sexual desires, it will ruin our relationship with God, as he sees all things. Is some brief, immediate gratification worth losing the most precious relationship we can have, with God? Moreover, nothing stays hidden forever, and the wife will eventually discover this dirty secret sinful life.

Proverbs 5:22-23 Updated American Standard Version (UASV)

22 The errors[37] of the wicked ensnare him,
   and he is held in the cords of his sin.
23 He will die for lack of discipline,
   and because of his great folly he will go astray.

An unwise person lacks discipline, the ability to control oneself. His fleshly desires lead his life. His wife no longer captivates this foolish young man, as he is spellbound by his own sinful desires, which lead him to ruination.

---

[37] **Error**: (Heb., ʾāwōn; Gr. anomia, paranomia) The Hebrew word awon essentially relates to erring, acting illegally or wrongly. This aspect of sin refers to committing a perverseness, wrongness, lawlessness, law breaking, which can also include the rejection of the sovereignty of God. It also focuses on the liability or guilt of one's wicked, wrongful act. This error may be deliberate or accidental; either willful deviation of what is right or unknowingly making a mistake. (Lev. 4:13-35; 5:1-6, 14-19; Num. 15:22-29; Ps 19:12-13) Of course, if it is intentional; then, the consequence is far more serious. (Num. 15:30-31) Error is in opposition to the truth, and those willfully sinning corrupt the truth, a course that only brings forth flagrant sin. (Isa 5:18-23) We can be hardened by the deceitfulness of sin.–Ex 9:27, 34-35; Heb. 3:13-15.

WIVES 5 What Does Wifely Subjection Mean?

Ephesians 5:22 Updated American Standard Version (UASV)

²² Wives, be **in subjection to your own husbands**, as to the Lord. ²³ For **the husband is the head of the wife**, as Christ also is the head of the congregation,³⁸

As we can see in the above, the Word of God clearly states at Ephesians 5:22, "Wives, be **in subjection to your own husbands**, as to the Lord." What does it mean to be in subjection? Must a wife slavishly submit to every demand from her husband, regardless? Can she never act on your own and make decisions without the help or advice of her husband? Can she never think for herself, or believe differently from her husband?

In order to answer these questions, let us look at a Bible account of a woman, Abigail, who acted wisely when she went against her husband, Nabal. David was God's chosen king of Israel. The people of Israel and King David showed great kindness to Nabal. Yet, Nabal addressed them angrily and screamed at them, when King David made a request. King David did not take this well, he was going to deal harshly with this Nabal. Abigail realized how she, her husband and the whole household were in grave danger. She got King David to turn back from his anger.–1 Samuel 25:2-35.

Abigail admitted to David that her husband was a worthless man. She then helped David and his men out with the provisions they had asked for, which Nabal had withheld. Now, under normal circumstances, a loving wife should never publicly say something demeaning about her husband. Was Abigail wrong in speaking

---

³⁸ Gr *ekklesia* ("assembly")

poorly of her husband? No, in this instance, she was saving her life, the lives of those in the house, and the life of her worthless husband. There is nothing in God's Word, which shows outside of this one time; Abigail made it a practice to talking badly about others. The account is also clear that Nabal did not complain about how Abigail handled things. However, in this situation, Godly wisdom meant that she needed to act on her own, making the decision, without the help or advice of her husband. Lastly, the Bible praises Abigail for her actions.– 1 Samuel 25:3, 25, 32-33.

Discernment Needed

It is not a good thing for a wife to feel as though she is pressured to do anything that is unwise or contrary to God's Word, simply because she is in subjection to her husband. In addition, she should not be made to feel guilty for taking the initiative in some essential matter, as was true of Abigail, not to mention Sarah with Abraham, in the case of Hagar and Ishmael.–Genesis 21:11-12.

The wife being in subjection to her husband is not an absolute obligation that she must comply with everything her husband says. How do we determine the difference? When the right principles are at stake, she may choose to disagree with her husband. However, this is no license to reject everything he says because the wife is falling back on this Scriptural principle here (bypassing the husband out of willfulness, spite, or other wrong motives). It is similar to the license to drive. As a licensed driver, you obey all the traffic laws. The laws gave you while you are on the road. But if a child walks out in front of you, you would choose to swerve so as to miss the child, even if it meant breaking the traffic laws, like going into the other lane or driving up on the sidewalk. This freedom, liberty to ignore the traffic laws in such an incidence does not give you the right to start ignoring minor traffic laws as you see fit. Lastly, even on the occasions when you show initiative or choose to disagree with your husband, you still do so in a godly manner.

The Husband Who Ignores His Headship

Under the direction of God's Word, it is the wife's goal and spirit of subjection that she cooperates with her husband, supporting the decisions that he makes. This is not burdensome if her husband is a spiritually mature Christian. If he is not, it can be a challenge.

If the husband is spiritually immature, how can the wife deal with this? Until the husband rightly assumes his role as the head of the house, she can offer her insights as suggestions on how to benefit the family. It is as though she is steering the relationship and slowly letting him take over the driving as he becomes more skilled in his role as the husband. However, continually nagging the husband would not be in line with the wife's biblical subjection. (Prov. 21:19) However, if the husband's poor decision is putting the family in jeopardy in any way, she may choose to follow the course that keeps the family safe.

Then, there is the wife who is married to the unbeliever, which raises the wifely subject to an even greater challenge. Nevertheless, she should remain in subjection as long as the Word of God is not being violated and the family is in no sort of jeopardy. If the husband does ask her to violate God's Law, she would, "obey God rather than men."–Acts 5:29

Even wives and husbands that feel they have a good understanding of Scripture, both can overstep their role within the family at times. The husband may lack concern and thoughtfulness in his decision making; the wife may press too hard to have her own way. How can they avoid this? It is by developing the quality of selflessness, where they do not put too much emphasis on self, as "we all stumble many times."–James 3:2.

Most men are very appreciative of a wife who shows initiative if it is done thoughtfully. Also, the level of cooperation is improved if both apologize when they make fall short due to human imperfection. We must remember how many times a day we sin against God, and he forgives us readily each time we ask.—Psalm 130:3-4.

WIVES 6 Strengthen Your Marriage Through Good Communication

The wife should make the husband happier each day, and her love should comfort him in difficult times. A husband should love his wife so much that he would rather spend time with her than anyone else. As the years pass in your marriage, never let difficult times cause you to go without communicating your love. Good communication will grow the trust between you and your wife, making the bond even stronger. Good communication will draw the two of you closer to God each day as well.

This first paragraph is a realistic expectation. There will be communication problems at times because you and your husband are different in so many ways and human imperfect and human weaknesses are still upon you. (Rom. 3:23) The two of you came from different cultures even if you were raised in the same country. There are some, who get married to someone from another country, who even speaks a different language. Therefore, you undoubtedly will have different ways of communicating. If you are going to communicate well, it will take much work on the part of the both of you.

Yes, all strong marriages that last forever take hard work, but it will bring great joy and pleasure to you and your wife. (Eccl. 9:9) Consider the love of Isaac and Rebekah from the Bible. (Gen. 24:67) The Scriptures show that they kept the love alive in their marriage for many decades. We see couples on news channels today being celebrated because they have been married for 70-80 years. How have they been able to accomplish this? They have grown or matured as a couple to the point where they can talk about their thoughts and feelings in an honest but kind way. They have developed the biblical qualities of understanding, love, respect, and humility.

Showing Understanding

Proverbs 16:20 Updated American Standard Version (UASV)

20 The one **who understands** a matter finds success,
and blessed is he who trusts in Jehovah.

Max Anders writes, "Trusting God translates into attentiveness to his words. The two parts of this verse make clear that the person who trusts in the LORD is the one who ponders or takes note of the word of instruction which God gives."[39] Think this through; so that you have understanding, the differences between a man and a woman are on purpose by the Creator. Men, do not be angered that your wife is so different. God made man and woman complement each other. This means that man and women were made different so they could complete each other. This explains why women communicate differently than men. It is true; most women love to talk about how they feel, their friends and family, the different personal things of life. Men, having a loving and honest communication will help your wife to feel loved. It is also true that many men do not like talking about their feelings, and would rather talk about activities, problems, and solutions. Men also desire respect. Remember, these are inborn characteristics, God-given.

If you are going to communicate well, it will take much work on the part of the both of you. Understanding is the only thing that will shine a light on how these differences actually help the husband and wife to complement each other. You and your husband are

---

[39] Anders, Max. Holman Old Testament Commentary - Proverbs (p. 96). B&H Publishing. Kindle Edition.

mentally wired differently on purpose, so as to balance each other as counterparts. However, your husband being the analytical man that he is, he is likely thinking, "if we are made different on purpose, why must I learn to listen and even talk about my feelings if God made us this way?" Yes, this is very insightful on his part, which is what gets you into trouble with his wife. God made man and woman perfect, with their characteristics and qualities balanced just right. However, once sin came into the world (Gen. 3:1-6, Rom. 3:23; 5:12) so that both man and woman are missing the mark of perfection and these characteristics and qualities became out of balance. It is by Holy Spirit, the mind of Christ, and a biblical mindset that the husband and wife have, which can get them back into balance.

In many cases, the husband is ready to offer solutions to the problem the moment he hears it rather than listen to his wife, who wants to be heard. This is very frustrating to the wife because he will cut her off and offer his superficial advice on what the two of you should do. The husband is looking for a solution; the wife is trying to express her feelings. The husband is simply looking for a quick solution to the problem. The husband should learn in time that his wife only wants him to listen to her.

Proverbs 18:13 Updated American Standard Version (UASV)

13 If one gives an answer before he hears,
 it is his folly and shame.

On this verse, Max Anders writes, "Jumping to conclusions is a special temptation for the self-important. They announce the solution before they have fully heard the problem. This is often a symptom of people who are arrogant, unteachable, or prejudiced. They have no interest in hearing the facts or anything else that might contradict their opinions."[40] Once the husband understands his wife's feelings, he will treat her in such a way that she feels loved. He must listen, really listen, so she knows that her feeling is important to him. (1 Pet. 3:7) The wife, in turn, will do her very best to understand better how he thinks. When you and your husband follow Bible principles, you will make wise decisions together, leading to a long happy marriage.

Wise King Solomon writes, "There is an appointed time for everything ... a time to be silent and a time to speak." (Eccl. 3:1, 7) In time, your wife will learn the best times to bring certain things up and other times not to mention certain things at all. For example, you might be overwhelmed with work, stressed about things, so she holds off telling you something until a better time. Solomon also wrote, "Like apples of gold in silver settings is a word spoken at the right time." (Prov. 25:11) On this, Anders writes, "An appropriate, well-timed saying can be as attractive and valuable as a fine piece of metalwork, apples of gold in settings of silver. Note that the apples are enhanced by the fine setting, just as the saying is "apt" precisely because it comes in the right context, carefully timed for the situation."[41]

It is not enough that the husband learns to listen attentively to his wife; he must also learn to talk about his own feelings. He, in time, will learn to tell his wife what is deep inside his heart. In time, he will find that while he is still a little uncomfortable talking about his problems, doing so will make him feel better, as he is getting it off his chest and sharing the burden with the one who loves and supports him most, his wife. He

---

[40] Anders, Max. Holman Old Testament Commentary - Proverbs (p. 211). B&H Publishing. Kindle Edition.

[41] Anders, Max. Holman Old Testament Commentary - Proverbs (p. 210). B&H Publishing. Kindle Edition.

needs to go to God in prayer, asking for the right words when talking with his wife.

Being that you and your husband are different and inherited sin has misaligned your good characteristics and qualities, you will have to work hard to change the way you communicate. You need to grow the desire to be more effective in your communication skills. The irony is man will spend hundreds if not thousands of hours becoming a more effective communicator in his witnessing to strangers, as a part of his ministry. Yet, he can be slow to do the same thing to the most important person in his life. As long as God is central, things will get better in the communication.–Psalm 127:1.

Growing Your Love for One Another

Love is the most important quality in a marriage. Paul said, "above all these things put on love, which is a perfect bond of union." (Col. 3:14) "Without love, all the other virtues may amount to mere moralism and little else (a thought found also in 1 Cor. 13:1–3). When love is present, there is harmony and unity in the community. It is not clear whether **love** binds the virtues together, completing a lovely garment of Christlike character, or whether **love** binds the members of the community together in mature oneness. Perhaps the ambiguity is intentional. Both ideas make good sense."[42] Love also binds the husband and wife together in mature oneness.

You and your husband need to continue to make an effort to learn more about each other. "Looking out for our own interests comes naturally. We need, and receive, no instruction for that. We are instructed to look out for **the interests of others**. We are to keep an eye out to discover ways we can help others even when they do not

---

[42] Max Anders, *Galatians-Colossians*, vol. 8, Holman New Testament Commentary (Nashville, TN: Broadman & Holman Publishers, 1999), 331.

see they need such help. The apostle stated in Galatians 6:2: "Carry each other's burdens, and in this way, you will fulfill the law of Christ."[43] Yes, we especially need to look out for the interests of our spouse.

Growing Your Respect for One Another

This book is about making your marriage the best that it can be by way of God's Word. However, we are also dealing with realistic expectations. Even the happiest marriage is not perfect. If you speak harshly to your wife, you are not **showing her the respect** that she deserves. If there is no respect, the marriage is doomed.

James 3:7-10, 17-18 Updated American Standard Version (UASV)

[7] For every kind[44] of beast and bird, of reptile and sea creature, can be tamed and has been tamed by mankind. [8] But no man can tame the tongue; it is a restless evil, full of deadly poison. [9] With it we bless our Lord[45] and Father, and with it we curse men who are made in the likeness of God. [10] from the same mouth come both blessing and cursing. My brothers, these things ought not to be so. [17] But the wisdom from above is first pure, then peaceable, gentle, reasonable, full of mercy and good fruits, impartial, without hypocrisy. [18] And the fruit of righteousness is sown in peace by[46] those who make peace.

---

[43] Max Anders, *Galatians-Colossians*, vol. 8, Holman New Testament Commentary (Nashville, TN: Broadman & Holman Publishers, 1999), 225.

[44] Lit., "*nature*"

[45] Gr., *ton Kurion*

[46] Or *for*; or possibly *among*

3:7–8. Verse 7 mentions four classifications of earthly animals men have subdued or tamed: animals which could walk, fly, crawl, or swim. Genesis 9:2 follows the same type of classification. These classifications represent a human observation about different types of animals rather than a scientific ordering.

Certainly no one has ever tamed a rhinoceros or an alligator, but in general wild animals can be brought under human control. Elephants, charmed snakes, and porpoises are examples of this principle. Although human beings can tame animals, they cannot tame their own tongues. The tongue is **a restless evil,** always busy creating more mischief. We must always keep the tongue under careful guard and never give it freedom to roam relentlessly, for it is **full of deadly poison.** Like the tongue of a serpent, the tongue deals out death (see Ps. 140:3).

Several years ago at the conclusion of a moving musical presentation, a man claiming to be Leonard Bernstein, Jr., son of the world-famous conductor, gave a check for twenty thousand dollars to the sanctuary choir of a large Baptist church. With tears in his eyes the man indicated that he and his father were Christian Jews and members of a New York City Baptist church. He asked that the church use the money to take the church choir to New York to perform with the New York Philharmonic Orchestra. Officials at the bank on which the check was drawn could not locate the account. The office of Leonard Bernstein in New York indicated that he had one son, whose name was Alexander. Neither father nor son had any connection with a Baptist church in New York. Someone had pulled a hoax. He had presented a picture of a tongue full of restless mischief.

The Bible's accurate picture of the tongue's destructive potential offers us no excuse for acquiescing to the tongue's evil potential (see Eph. 4:29). By committing our tongues to the power of God, we can see them used to build up and strengthen others rather than to tear them down.

Recently I spoke to a church in South Texas and focused during one evening on Paul's prayer in Ephesians 1:15–23. I urged my listeners to adopt the requests of Paul's prayer as they interceded for others. The next day one of the members pulled me aside to say that those words from Paul had changed her own prayer life. Her words of encouragement built me up and sent me back to my teaching with renewed enthusiasm. A tongue committed to God can be used as a positive tool for building hope and stamina in others.

3:9–10. Verse 9 mentions both a positive and a negative use of the tongue. The positive use involved praise of God, the highest function of human speech (see Ps. 103:1–5). The negative use involved cursing human beings. Cursing refers to personal verbal abuse, perhaps arising from loss of temper in an argument or debate. It also involves the expression of angry wishes on enemies. It includes speech which is insulting as well as profane.

Verse 10 spotlights the inconsistency of this action. We are sinfully inconsistent when we bless God and then curse those made in God's likeness. When we curse those whom God has made, we are effectively cursing God. He is the object of both expressions. Such a double standard is outrageous: **My brethren, this should not be.**

3:17. True wisdom is free from self-interest and strife. This verse lists eight traits or characteristics of true wisdom. The first is purity. People with true wisdom are **pure** in that they have put aside the vices of a self-seeking nature and factionalism. This trait provides the secure foundation for all that follows.

The following five traits show the attitude of true wisdom toward other people. **Peace-loving** means it demonstrates a desire to promote peace between struggling factions. **Considerate** refers to being reasonable in the demands it makes on others. **Submissive** indicates a willingness to learn from others by being open to reason. **Full of mercy** is revealed by offering compassion to those in distress. **Full of good fruit** is shown by kind actions and helpful deeds to others.

The final two traits describe the essential nature of true wisdom in itself. It is **impartial,** without prejudice and unwavering in its commitments. True wisdom is **sincere,** genuine and open in its approaches to others. Jesus particularly showed his genuineness in his dialogues with Pilate (John 18:33–37).

3:18. Verse 18 concludes this section with a description of the effects of true wisdom. True wisdom results in **a harvest of righteousness,** that is, a conformity to God's will. True wisdom also lets one experience **peace,** the enjoyment of harmonious relationships between human beings.

Over the years Christians in various churches have developed wide differences in their social practices. American Christians from the South sometimes oppose mixed swimming, but they may offend a Christian from the North by their cultivation and use of tobacco. Christians differ in their preferences for English versions of the Bible. Some regard the use of certain modern translations as sure signs of compromise and moral apostasy. European Christians live in a culture which more readily accepts the use of alcohol by believers. Many American Christians find it hard to tolerate this acceptance. American women almost never feel compelled to wear a covering for their heads to worship services. Among many eastern European Christian groups it is expected that women will wear a covering, even if it is only a scarf. Each of these circumstances demands a response of peace and consideration to prevent strife, factionalism, and petty quarreling.[47]

Growing Your Humility

It is only possible for you and your wife to communicate in a kind and loving way you are, "humble minded." (1 Pet. 3:8) Humility will get you through the difficulties because it moves you to say, "I'm sorry." At times, the words "I'm sorry" can be more important than the words, "I love you." When you and your wife pray together focus on how you sin against God every day, and yet God forgives you every day, as long as you are truly repentant and remorseful.

Pride will only lead to the ruination of marriage. A proud person is incapable of saying, "I'm sorry, please forgive me." A proud person likes to keep score as to who said what and who started an argument. The proud person likes to make excuses, or blaming another person instead of owning the mistake, rationalizing and justifying. A proud person is not after peace as this one only gets louder trying to rationalize the mistake that led to the argument. (Eccl. 7:9) The proud person will also abandon the conversation because the other person is the one that was wrong, as opposed to saying, "I'm sorry, please forgive me." James tells us, "God opposes the proud, but gives grace to the humble."[48] (Jam. 4:6) Yes, pride will not only ruin a marriage but also your relationship with God.

When you and your husband disagree, it is best to loving and respectfully work to solve the problem quickly instead of being proud, and ignoring the

---

[47] Thomas D. Lea, *Hebrews, James*, vol. 10, Holman New Testament Commentary (Nashville, TN: Broadman & Holman Publishers, 1999), 304-305, 307–308.

[48] A quotation from Pro 3:34

problem. The reason the same problem is never solved and keep rearing its ugly head is, there is never an understanding of what the problem is. Paul said, "Be angry, and yet do not sin;[49] do not let the sun go down on your anger, **27** nor give place[50] to the devil." (Eph. 4:26-27) Going to bed with a heavy heart, to rise in the morning to a distressed mind and spirit, this will cause a separation and a lessening of love eventually. It is best to try and solve the problem quickly in a loving, peaceful, respectful way. If a resolution cannot be met, it is best to hug, hold each other and express your love. This way you go to bed knowing all will be well.

Ashley Murrell, 33, had [an argument] with her husband Mikey, 36, a carpet cleaner, about his long working hours after he returned home late from a 16-hour shift.

The mother-of-three told him to sleep on the sofa after the argument, but when she woke up the next morning, she discovered that he was dead.

She later learned that he had been working extra hours to earn enough money to take her to Prague for their wedding anniversary on July 3.[51]

Good communication is when you and your wife can speak to each other, openly, without fear, honestly but kindly and respectfully about your thoughts and feelings. You have an understanding of your spouse when

---

[49] A reference to Ps 4:4

[50] Or *an opportunity* to the devil

[51] Woman whose husband died after she banished him to the sofa ... https://www.yahoo.com/news/woman-whose-husband-died-banished-sofa-found-love-brother-081433639.html (July 12, 2017)

you truly know how she feels and you meet her needs, as she meets your needs.

WIVES 7 How to Compromise

Let us say that you and your wife a different preferences on the amount of money that you will spend on a household item. There are only three options to reach a resolution.

First, you can be stubborn until you get your way, or the wife could be stubborn until she gets her own way. **Second**, you could passively submit without discussing or resisting, to your spouse's wishes. **Third**, you and your husband could compromise.

Some feel that compromise is a sign of weakness, which would be a case of pride if you feel that way. Or, others might feel like no one is getting what they want in a compromise.

Understand this comprising need not be a lose-lose situation, but rather it can be done right so that it is a win-win situation. However, before we look at the world of compromising, we need to look at a few things involved in this skill.

What You Need to Know

Teamwork is involved in compromising. It is true; before you were married, you made all of your decisions based on your own view of the pros and cons of a choice. Now, there is the most important person in the world, who is equally involved in this decision-making process, and you must put your marriage above your personal preferences. This is actually not a negative but rather an advantage. You have likely heard it said, "Two minds are better than one." This is because **two minds have a better chance** of finding the best decision than just one mind alone that may not consider all the evidence. The husband will have insight that you may not have considered and you might have insights that he has not considered.

You must be **open-minded** if the compromise is going to be successful as a win-win situation. Sure, you are not going to agree with everything your husband says or believes and nor will she agree with everything either. Nevertheless, you have to be truly willing to accept his way, and he has to be truly open to the possibility of your way. If you are sitting there with your arms folded, thinking of rebuttals to everything he says before he even finishes his points, even shaking your head no, there will be no successful compromise.

You must be ready to be **self-sacrificing** if the compromise is going to be successful. You have also likely heard the saying, "it's either my way or the highway." No husband will want to spend his life with the ultimatum, which indicates he will either conform to the desires of his wife or else be excluded. This compromise will only work if both are self-sacrificing, i.e., giving up some things for the other. Marriage is a bit of giving and taking, not just take.

How to Compromise Correctly

You must begin the conversation by **setting the right tone**, or it will end before it ever begins. If you voice gets louder as you defend your preference, or you resort to harsh words, the likelihood of ending with a successful compromise is very slim. The apostle Paul writes "put on as God's chosen ones, holy and beloved, a heart of compassion, kindness, humility, meekness, and patience." (Col. 3:12) You need to acquire and use such qualities if you and your husband are going to avoid arguing.

Each person should be given the **opportunity to fully explain** why they feel the way they do, without being interrupted, without eye rolling, without the other shaking their head, without the other sitting with their arms folded. Once both have fully explained the reason for their preference, you need to **search for common**

ground. Instead of focusing on where your preferences differ, focus in on where they agree.

Finding Common Ground

The two of you need to have a tablet and pen. You and your husband need to make two lists. In the first list, write down the aspects of your choice that you feel most strongly about. In the second list, write down those things that you could give up. After you, both have your list, look them over together, make a list of aspects that you both agree on that you both feel strongest about. Then, work your way through the parts where you both feel you could give ground. The most important thing is having all possible aspects on paper, so you can evaluate more clearly, what can be compromised.

Some issues will be easy to settle, and this process will not be needed. If they are more complex use this process. Also, brainstorm between the two of you to find a solution without having to begin this process. Wise King Solomon wrote, "Two are better than one because they have a good reward for their efforts."–Ecclesiastes 4:9, CSB.

You must have a willing heart that will adjust its view. You must be willing to listen to your wife objectively. Paul Wrote, "let each one of you love his wife as himself, and let the wife see that she respects her husband." (Eph. 5:33, ESV) If both you and your husband truly love and respect each other, you will be willing to consider each other's viewpoint.

Colossians 4:6 Updated American Standard Version (UASV)

Let your speech always be gracious, seasoned with salt, so that you may know how you ought to answer each person.

WIVES 8 What Does Subjection in Marriage Mean?

The Christian woman that marries will have to make many adjustments. The one that might affect her most will touch on her liberty. Before you married your husband, you were free to make the decisions about your life yourself. You need not consult anyone if you did not want. Now that you are married, you are now obligated to consult your husband and get permission on major decisions that you formerly decided. Why is this so?

Because the Creator of humanity created man first and then he created woman as the complement of the man. He assigned the man the role as the head of the wife and the future children. The feminist today "is a philosophy emphasizing the patriarchal roots of inequality between men and women, or, more specifically, social dominance of women by men. Radical feminism views patriarchy as dividing rights, privileges, and power primarily by gender, and as a result oppressing women and privileging men."[52] This has caused a severe crisis the God-ordained family arrangement of Christians. "Christian feminism is an aspect of feminist theology, which seeks to advance and understand the equality of men and women morally, socially, spiritually, and in leadership from a Christian perspective. Christian feminists argue that contributions by women in that direction are necessary for a complete understanding of Christianity."[53] This is one reason for the high divorce rates among Christian families that we

---

[52] Accessed July 12, 2017 https://www.thoughtco.com/what-is-radical-feminism-3528997

[53] Harrison, Victoria S. "Modern Women, Traditional Abrahamic Religions and Interpreting Sacred Texts." *Feminist Theology: The Journal of the Britain & Ireland School of Feminist Theology* 15.2 (2007):145-159.

see today. In any organized group of people, from a nation to a family, someone has to have the final decision.

Ephesians 5:22 Updated American Standard Version (UASV)

²² Wives, be in subjection to your own husbands, as to the Lord.

The apostle Paul here and in verse 23 emphasizes subjection and respect. Yes, a wife is in subjection to her husband but this in no way means that she is inferior to her husband. Every living person in heaven and on earth is subject to someone. It is up to the husband to carry out his headship in a proper manner.

---

22 Within the marriage relationship wives[200] are addressed first, and they are urged to be subordinate to their[201] husbands as to the Lord. Although the verse does not contain any verb, 'submit' carries over from v. 21, with the imperative being understood instead of the participle.[202] The notion of submission in the preceding

---

[200] Here the nominative case with the article (αἱ γυναῖκες), rather than the vocative, is used in address (cf. BDF §147[3]). It is 'wives' who are in view, not women generally.

[201] Although the adjective ἴδιος originally signified what was 'one's own', by New Testament times it differed little from a reflexive or possessive pronoun. In this context it is rendered 'their husbands' (so BAGD, 369; Bruce, 384; Schnackenburg, 246; and Best, 532).

[202] The verb 'submit' does not appear in the best Greek text, so that the verse is dependent for its sense on the participle of v. 21. This is the reading of 𝔓⁴⁶ B Clement Origen and several Greek mss. according to Jerome. Other textual traditions supply some form of ὑποτάσσειν ('submit') before or after τοῖς ἰδίοις ἀνδράσιν ('their husbands'), such as ὑποτάσσεσθε ('be subject') or ὑποτασσέσθωσαν ('let them be subject'). Most editors argue for the omission of the verb because it is the shorter reading and it is likely that later scribes included the verb for the sake of clarity. For a detailed discussion, see B. M. Metzger, *Textual Commentary*, 608–9.

verse is now unpacked without repeating the verb.[203] As we have already seen, the keyword rendered 'submit' has to do with the subordination of someone in an ordered array to another who is above the first, that is, in authority over that person. At the heart of this submission is the notion of 'order'. God has established certain leadership and authority roles within the family, and submission is a humble recognition of that divine ordering. The apostle is not urging every woman to submit to every man, but wives to their husbands. The use of the middle voice of this verb (cf. Col. 3:18) emphasizes the voluntary character of the submission. Paul's admonition to wives is an appeal to free and responsible persons which can only be heeded voluntarily, never by the elimination or breaking of the human will, much less by means of a servile submissiveness.[204]

The idea of subordination to authority in general, as well as in the family, is out of favour in a world which prizes permissiveness and freedom. Christians are often affected by these attitudes. Subordination smacks of exploitation and oppression that are deeply resented. But authority is not synonymous with tyranny, and the submission to which the apostle refers does not imply inferiority. Wives and husbands (as well as children and parents, servants and masters) have different God-appointed roles, but all have equal dignity because they have been made in the divine image and in Christ have

---

[203] D. B. Wallace, *Greek Grammar*, 659.

[204] Cf. Barth, 609. M. J. Harris, *Colossians and Philemon* (Grand Rapids: Eerdmans, 1991), 178, comments: 'It is a case of voluntary submission in recognition of the God-appointed leadership of the husband and the divinely ordained hierarchical order in creation (cf. 1 Cor. 11:3–9)'.

put on the new person who is created to be like God (4:24).[205] Having described the single new humanity which God is creating in his Son, with its focus on the oneness in Christ of all, especially Jew and Gentile (cf. Col. 3:11; Gal. 3:28), the apostle 'does not now [in this household table] destroy his own thesis by erecting new barriers of sex, age and rank in God's new society in which they have been abolished'.[206] That the verb 'submit, be subordinate' can be used of Christ's submission to the authority of the Father (1 Cor. 15:28) shows that it can denote a functional subordination without implying inferiority, or less honour and glory.[207]

The motivation for the wife to be subject to her husband is spelled out in the final phrase, *as to the Lord*.[208] The general admonition of v. 21 to be submissive in 'the fear of Christ' finds concrete expression for the wife in the marriage situation: as she is subordinate to her husband, so in that very action she is submitting to the Lord. Her voluntary response is not called for because of her role in society, nor is it to be understood as separate from her submission to Christ. Rather, it is part and parcel of the way that she serves the Lord Jesus (cf. Col. 3:23 of servants who engage in wholehearted work for their

---

[205] 'Equality of *worth* is not identity of *role*', J. H. Yoder, cited by Stott, 218.

[206] Stott, 217. Note his timely discussion of v. 22 in the light of contemporary attitudes (215–20).

[207] Against the view of G. Bilezikian, 'Hermeneutical Bungee-Jumping: Subordination in the Godhead', *JETS* 40 (1997), 57–68.

[208] 'Lord' (κύριος) is not a reference to her husband, as some have claimed. The plural 'to their lords' (τοῖς κυρίοις) would have been written to correspond to 'to their husbands' (τοῖς ἰδίοις ἀνδράσιν).

masters and in that very action serve their heavenly Lord).[54]

Ephesians 5:23 Updated American Standard Version (UASV)

[23] For **the husband is the head of the wife**, as Christ also is the head of the congregation,[55] he himself being the Savior of the body.

Again, this verse is not a license to abuse or dominate the wife. It does mean that the husband has the final say in everything as long as he does not require the wife to break God's law. However, only the foolish husband would not consider the insights of his wife. When she is correct, humbly accept her direction. A husband may feel that headship permits him to absolute control. However, this is not so. His wife, though in subjection, is not his slave. She is a complement. (Gen. 2:18)

---

23 The reason for the wife's submission to her husband is now expressed through the causal clause: 'for the husband is head of the wife as Christ also is head of the church'. On two earlier occasions in Ephesians the key term 'head' has been used, both with reference to Christ (1:22; 4:15). Now, for the first time, the husband's headship is stated as a fact, and made the basis of his wife's submission. The origin of this headship is not elaborated here, although in the fuller treatments of 1 Corinthians 11:3–12 and 1 Timothy 2:11–13 it is grounded in the order of creation, especially the narrative of Genesis 2 (cf. 1 Cor. 11:8, 9).

---

[54] Peter Thomas O'Brien, *The Letter to the Ephesians*, The Pillar New Testament Commentary (Grand Rapids, MI: W.B. Eerdmans Publishing Co., 1999), 411–412.

[55] Gr *ekklesia* ("assembly")

In each of the earlier instances of this term in Ephesians it signifies 'head' as 'ruler' or 'authority',[209] rather than 'source',[210] or one who is 'prominent, preeminent'.[211] At 1:22 'head' expresses the idea of Christ's supremacy and authority over the cosmos, especially the evil powers, which he exercises on behalf of the church (cf. Col. 1:18; 2:10). His rule over his people is described at 4:15, and this headship is expressed in his care and nourishment, as well as in his leadership of them in the fulfilment of the divine purposes.[212] Here the headship of the husband, in the light of the usage at 1:22,

---

[209] So W. Grudem, 'Does *kephalē* ('head') Mean "Source" or "Authority Over" in Greek Literature? A Survey of 2,336 Examples', *TrinJ* 6 (1985), 38–59; and 'The Meaning of Κεφαλή ('Head'): A Response to Recent Studies', *TrinJ* 11 (1990), 3–72. Note the summary of the debate by J. A. Fitzmyer, 'Kephale in 1 Corinthians 11:3', *Int* 47 (1993), 52–59; see also the detailed discussion of G. W. Dawes, *The Body*, 122–49, who concludes that κεφαλή is used as a metaphor indicating 'authority over'. Only in this verse in Ephesians, however, does the term have 'two distinct referents', namely, Christ and the husband.

[210] Advocates of the meaning 'source' include S. Bedale, 'The Meaning of κεφαλή in the Pauline Epistles', *JTS* 5 (1954), 211–15; G. D. Fee, *1 Corinthians*, 502–5; C. C. Kroeger, '*Head*', 267–83; and *DPL*, 375–77.

[211] A. Perriman, *Speaking of Women*, 13–33, who rejects both 'source, origin' and 'leadership, authority over' as meanings for κεφαλή, argues in favour of the term signifying 'prominence' or 'pre-eminence'. He acknowledges that this may 'also entail authority and leadership', but 'it is a mistake to include this as part of the common denotation of the term' (31; cf. Hoehner). This interpretation, however, runs into difficulties with the expression 'Christ is head of the church' (Paul is saying more than that Christ is pre-eminent in relation to the church, though this is true), while his exegesis of vv. 23–24 (55–57) is not convincing. The ἀλλά ('but') in v. 24 does not signify a change of emphasis from headship (v. 23), which only has to do with prominence and preeminence, to subordination with its notions of authority over others. Instead, the adversative ἀλλά ('but') provides a contrast with the preceding clause, 'he himself is the Saviour of the body' (v. 23c), which is not true of the husband's relationship to his wife (see on v. 24).

[212] C. E. Arnold, 'Jesus Christ', 365.

the general context of the authority structure of the Graeco-Roman household,[213] and the submission of the wife to her husband within marriage in vv. 22–24,[214] refers to his having authority over his wife; thus he is her leader or ruler.[215]

The mere presence of the terms 'head' and 'submission' in this context does not of itself 'establish stereotypes of masculine and feminine behaviour'.[216] Different cultures may assign different roles for men and women, husbands and wives. What is important here is that the nature of the husband's headship in God's new society is explained in relation to Christ's headship. The husband is head of the wife *as also*[217] Christ is head of the church. 'Although [Paul] ... grounds the fact of the husband's headship in creation, he defines it in relation to the headship of Christ the redeemer'.[218] Christ's headship

---

[213] For recent discussions of authority structures in the Graeco-Roman family see Lincoln, 357–59; and Hoehner.

[214] Cf. Lincoln, 369.

[215] Note the discussion of the lexical semantics of this, together with several criticisms of the view that 'head' means 'source', in P. Cotterell and M. Turner, *Linguistics and Biblical Interpretation* (London: SPCK, 1989), 141–45. They conclude that 'head' carries the sense of 'master' or 'lord'.

[216] Stott, 225.

[217] ὡς καί has comparative force, 'as also'. Cf. BAGD, 897; and Hoehner.

[218] Stott, 225. Contra Schnackenburg, 246, who acknowledges that Paul argues from creation in 1 Cor. 11, but considers this argument 'no longer convincing to us'. It loses its status in the light of Christ's headship, expressed in Eph. 5:23b. But if we assume that the 'author' of Ephesians is reflecting a view similar to that expressed in 1 Cor. 11, why should the words 'as Christ is head of the church' overthrow the husband's headship? It is better to speak of the latter being defined or explicated in the light of Christ's headship. K. H. Fleckenstein, *Ordnet euch einander unter in der Furcht Christi: Die Eheperikope in Eph 5, 21–33: Geschichte der Interpretation, Analyse und Aktualisierung des Textes* (Würzburg: Echter, 1994), 216, understands the role of the husband as

over the church is expressed by his loving it and giving his life for it, as vv. 25–27 so clearly show. This will have profound implications for the husband's behaviour as head of his wife (v. 28).

The additional words, 'he himself is the Saviour of the body', at first sight appear rather surprising and have caused exegetes to question whether they refer to the husband's role as his wife's protector or are part of the Christ-church/husband-wife analogy, thereby signifying that as Christ is the Saviour of the body, so also the husband is in some sense the saviour of his wife. While the term 'saviour' could possibly be taken in a general sense of protector or provider of the wife's welfare, so that the analogy of Christ's relationship to the church can be parallelled in the husband's 'saving' his wife, both syntax and usage are against it.

Instead, the clause is specifically focussed on Christ, not the husband: the personal pronoun 'he *himself*' is emphatic by its presence and position, and clearly refers to Christ. Nowhere in the context is the wife regarded as the husband's body as the church is Christ's body.[219] Further, the term 'saviour', which turns up twenty-four times in the New Testament, always refers to Jesus or God, but never to human beings.[220] To interpret the words, then, of Christ[221] fits appropriately within the flow

---

'head of the wife' to be derived from 'the patriarchal structure of the ancient family', but does not tie it to creation.

[219] The husband and the wife are 'one flesh' (5:31), and husbands are to love their wives 'as their own bodies', but this is a reference to the husbands' bodies, not the wives'.

[220] Of Jesus: Luke 2:11; John 4:42; Acts 5:31; 13:23; Phil. 3:20; 2 Tim. 1:10, etc. Of God: Luke 1:47; 1 Tim. 1:1; 2:3; 4:10, etc.

[221] The suggestions that 1 Cor. 7:16 (with its reference to the believing spouse being the instrument of the unbelieving spouse's salvation) and Tobit 6:18 (where Tobias marries his cousin Sarah to save her) provide significant parallels to the husband being the saviour of his

of the apostle's argument. Paul has been urging wives to be submissive to their husbands. The reason for this turns on the headship of the husband, which is parallel to Christ's headship or rule over the church. Paul then adds that the person who is head of the church is none other than the one who is the Saviour of the body. His saving activity, especially his sacrificial death (2:14–18; cf. 5:2), was for the deliverance of men and women in dire spiritual peril (2:1–10).

Later in the paragraph, the apostle will urge husbands as heads of their wives to serve them in love. Their pattern is the Lord Jesus, whose headship was demonstrated in his loving the church and giving himself up for it, in order to present it faultless to himself (vv. 25–27).[56]

Subjection Is Relative

The husband authority over his wife is not absolute. We can consider the wife's subject to the husband as a Christian is subject to the superior governing authorities. The apostle Paul said, "Let every soul[57] be in subjection to the governing authorities. For there is no authority except by God, and those that exist have been placed[58] by God." (Rom. 13:1) Yet, as Christian, while we obey the laws of the land, it is in conjunction with the Word of God. If any governmental authority asked us to do something that breaks God's law, we obey what Peter and the apostles said, "We must obey God rather than

---

wife have been shown to be unconvincing by Lincoln, 370, and Hoehner. Note the discussion in G. W. Dawes, *The Body*, 150.

[56] Peter Thomas O'Brien, *The Letter to the Ephesians*, The Pillar New Testament Commentary (Grand Rapids, MI: W.B. Eerdmans Publishing Co., 1999), 412–415.

[57] Or *person*

[58] Or *established, instituted*

men." (Ac 5:29) In a similar way, the wife is in subjection to her husband unless he is asking something of her that is against the Word of God.

1 Peter 3:1-2 Updated American Standard Version (UASV)

3 In the same way, you wives, be submissive to your own husbands so that even if any of them are disobedient to the word, they may be won without a word by the behavior of their wives, **2** as they observe your chaste and respectful behavior.

3:1. These words are addressed generally to all Christian wives, but with special attention to those women whose husbands are not believers in Jesus Christ. **In the same way** takes the reader back to something previously introduced. The manner of behavior is described with the words, **be submissive to your husbands.** Submission appeared first in 2:13 in reference to the believer's response to authority and again in verse 18 in discussing the slave's response to the master.

Opinions vary widely as to how these injunctions should be defined. One well-intentioned but misguided commentator says that "the meaning of the wife's submission to her husband concerns the sexual relationship and should not be taken in a more general and oppressive sense" (Hillyer, 92). Such an interpretation not only violates the meaning of the word but also violates the context of this verse. Submission is best understood as "to voluntarily yield your rights or will to someone else's wishes or advice, as an expression of love for that person." Another spin on the term would be to define it as simply considering the needs of your husband and fulfilling them (Marshall, 99).

In all discussions related to submission, if the wishes, desires, or needs of the husband involve a direct violation of the Word of God, then submission does not

---

apply. In such cases, to practice submission would involve violating the higher principle of obedience to God and his Word previously held out as the believer's goal (see 1:14–15, 22; 2:11).

Submitting oneself to another is the opposite of self-assertion, the opposite of an independent, autocratic spirit. It is the desire to get along with someone else. It involves being satisfied at times with less than what one may deserve or claim as a right. The goal of this type of behavior is to win over to Christ the non-believing husband. This occurs **without words.** This does not mean that a wife is never to speak, but rather that she is not to resort to constant arguments and nagging discussions. The husband will be more influenced by **the behavior** of his wife. This links this chapter to chapter 2, where verse 12 indicates that the non-Christian audience can be positively influenced for Christ as they observe the consistent and godly behavior of a believer.

As Christian wives live out the declaration of the praises of God, their husbands will be influenced. For the Christian wife living with a non-Christian husband, Peter's previous discussion of suffering even while doing what is right may have some application even within the context of her marriage and home. What a Christian wife says often will not change her husband; how she lives out her faith before him will make the difference.

3:2. Living a life of **purity and reverence** can make a difference. Purity signifies more than just moral or sexual purity, although this is included. The term suggests moral and ethical behavior that maintains a high standard. According to recent surveys, forty percent of the women polled by *USA Today* indicated that they have had extramarital affairs. Obviously, Peter's advice is still relevant today. Purity of life will generally not occur, however, unless "reverence" is also a part of it. The "reverence" is for the Lord and indicates a deep desire to keep his commandments. This desire to obey God should be the driving motive, resulting in a high moral standard.[59]

Ephesians 5:24 Updated American Standard Version (UASV)

[24] But as the congregation[60] is subject to Christ, so also the wives should be to their husbands in everything.

24 The church's submission to Christ is now presented as the model of the wife's submission to her husband. The exhortation to wives in v. 22 is repeated and reinforced with the addition of the words 'in everything'. Here, however, the sequence of v. 22 is reversed. The analogy of the church being subject to Christ is mentioned before the admonition that *wives should submit to their husbands in everything.*

Although the NIV's introductory *now* does not indicate it, the verse begins with the adversative conjunction 'but', which provides a contrast with the preceding clause, 'he himself is the Saviour of the body' (v. 23c).[222] This is not true of the husband's relationship

---

[59] David Walls and Max Anders, *I & II Peter, I, II & III John, Jude,* vol. 11, Holman New Testament Commentary (Nashville, TN: Broadman & Holman Publishers, 1999), 48–49.

[60] Gr *ekklesia* ("assembly")

NIV New International Version

[222] So the majority of commentators, including Calvin, Alford, Meyer, Abbott, M. Barth, Sampley, Schnackenburg, Lincoln, and Hoehner. This is better than regarding the ἀλλά as having resumptive ('consequently'; so Robinson, 124, 205; and Bruce, 385) or consecutive force (S. F. Miletic, *"One Flesh": Eph. 5.22–24, 5.31: Marriage and the New Creation* [Rome: Pontifical Biblical Institute, 1988], 102–3). The variations in the English versions ('therefore': AV; 'but': RV, ASV, NASB, NEB; 'and': TEV, JB, NJB; 'now': NIV; or the conjunction was left untranslated: RSV, NRSV) indicate something of the difficulties translators have had in understanding the force of the conjunction (so Hoehner).

to his wife. Although he has responsibility for her welfare, he is not her saviour (see on v. 23). So by means of the adversative 'but' (= 'notwithstanding this difference')[223] Paul makes the distinction between Christ and the husband, before comparing the church's submission to Christ with the wife's submission to her husband.[224] By using the same verb 'submit' (a middle voice in the original) the apostle stresses the willing character of the church's submission to Christ, and thus underscores what has already been asserted in v. 22 about the free and voluntary nature of the wife's subordination to her husband.

But what is involved in the church's submission to Christ, and what light does this throw on the wife's submission to her husband? The church's relationship to Christ is the focus of attention in several passages within Ephesians, and these spell out important facets of its submission to its Lord. God has graciously placed everything under Christ's feet and caused him to be head over all for the benefit of the church. The church gladly submits to his beneficent rule (1:22). Christ is the vital cornerstone on whom God's building is constructed. As this new community looks to Christ it grows and progresses to its ultimate goal of holiness (2:20, 21). Christ indwells the hearts of his people, establishing them so that they may be able to comprehend the greatness of his love (3:17, 19). The church receives Christ's gift of grace (4:7), and the ministers he gives for the purpose of enriching the whole body (4:11, 12). The church thus grows towards its head, the ultimate goal of which is the

---

223 Cf. Abbott, 166.

224 The comparative particle ὡς ('as') begins the comparison, and this is balanced by the adverbial particle οὕτως ('so') and the conjunction καί ('and') which introduce the second clause. Wives (αὐ γυναῖκες) are the subject of the admonition, and the present middle imperative ὑποτασσέσθωσαν ('let them be subordinate') needs to be supplied (A. T. Robertson, Greek Grammar, 394).

whole measure of Christ's fulness (v. 13), and it receives from him all that is necessary for this growth (vv. 15, 16). In submitting to its Lord, God's people had 'learned Christ': they welcomed him as a living person and were shaped by his teaching (v. 20). This involved submitting to his rule of righteousness and living by standards and values completely different from what they had known. The church is to imitate Christ's sacrificial love (5:2). It seeks to please its Lord (5:10) by living in goodness, holiness, and truth and by understanding his will (5:17). His people sing praises to him (5:19), and live in godly fear and awe of him (5:21). Accordingly, the church's submission to Christ means 'looking to its head for his beneficial rule, living by his norms, experiencing his presence and love, receiving from him gifts that will enable growth to maturity, and responding to him in gratitude and awe'.[225] It is these attitudes that the wife is urged to develop as she submits to her husband.

The additional element which reinforces this exhortation (cf. v. 22) is the concluding phrase, 'in everything'. In the Colossians household table the similar expression 'in everything' is used of the *obedience* of children to parents (Col. 3:20), and of slaves to masters (Col. 3:22; cf. Tit. 3:9). Although this phrase has raised modern questions about the *limitations* of a wife's submission to her husband (arising out of the contemporary desire to control the scope of someone's authority, specifying what decisions a person in authority can make),[226] 'in everything' indicates that the wife is to be subordinate to her husband *in every area of life*. In this sense it is all-encompassing, and is not, as some have

---

[225] Lincoln, 372. Cf. S. F. Miletic, *"One Flesh"*, 43, who aptly comments that 'the Christ/church relationship provides direction ("to the Lord"), perception (husband as "head" as Christ is "head") and example (church as paradigm) for the wife's act of subordination'.

[226] Rightly noted by S. B. Clark, *Man and Woman*, 83.

suggested, restricted to sexual matters or some other special sphere of their relationship. 'No part of her life should be outside of her relationship to her husband and outside of subordination to him'.[227] Just as the church is to submit to Christ in everything, so in every sphere wives are expected to submit to their husbands. The motivation for doing this is a true and godly reverence for Christ (5:21; cf. v. 33).

Furthermore, the exhortation to be subordinate 'in everything' should be read within the flow of the argument in the chapter. By God's design husband and wife are 'one flesh' (v. 31; Gen. 2:24), and the divine intention is that they should 'function together under one head, not as two autonomous individuals living together'.[228] This subordination of wife to husband 'has a practical aspect in that it creates a greater effectiveness in their working together as one'.[229] And it anticipates God's ultimate intention of bringing back all things into unity in Christ (1:10; see below).

The question, then, as to whether the wife is to submit to her husband regardless of what he commands is not addressed. But the words 'in everything', however they are interpreted, are not intended to reverse the instructions and exhortations already laid upon *all* believers in the paraenesis of Ephesians 4–6. This admonition to wives in the household table cannot be

---

[227] S. B. Clark, Man and Woman, 83. If 'in everything' refers to every sphere of the husband-wife relationship, then it confuses the issue to speak of 'complete obedience' or 'full and complete subordination' (as Lincoln, 373, does).

[228] G. W. Knight, 'Husbands and Wives as Analogues of Christ and the Church: Ephesians 5:21–33 and Colossians 3:18–19', in Recovering Biblical Manhood and Womanhood: A Response to Evangelical Feminism, ed. J. Piper and W. Grudem (Wheaton, IL: Crossway, 1991), 170. He adds that the wife's 'submission is coextensive with all aspects of their relationship'.

[229] S. B. Clark, Man and Woman, 81.

interpreted as a kind of grid through which all the earlier exhortations are filtered in the interests of serving the husband's authority.[230] Further, it goes without saying that wives are not to be subordinate in matters that are sinful or contrary to God's commands (cf. Acts 5:29).

There is no suggestion that this exhortation to be submissive is intended to stifle the wife's thinking or acting. She should not act unilaterally, but rather submit willingly to her husband's leadership. 'Just as the church should willingly submit to Christ in all things and, if it does so, will not find that stifling, demeaning, or stultifying of growth and freedom, so also wives should willingly submit to their husbands in all things and, if they do so, will not find that stifling, demeaning, or stultifying'.[231] As with the other admonitions in the household table, God sets forth these instructions for our good.

Accordingly, the wife's submission to her husband is *not conditional* on his loving her after the pattern of Christ's love or showing his unceasing care for her. Later the apostle will make it clear that husbands are not to rule their wives insensitively (vv. 25–27). Those in authority should not 'lord it over' those who are led (2 Cor. 1:24). But the wife's response of submission, which is not an unthinking obedience to his leadership, is to be rendered gladly, irrespective of whether the husband will heed the injunctions explicitly addressed to him or not. Contrary to much contemporary Western thinking, there is no suggestion that wives are to be submissive to their husbands only if their husbands are loving. We have

---

[230] Barth, 620–21, points out that 'in everything' cannot mean mere blind obedience, especially when it would mean acting contrary to God's commands. On the other hand, it is inappropriate to 'compil[e] a short or long list of exemptions to prove that "in everything" actually means "not in everything" ' (621)!

[231] G. W. Knight, 'Husbands and Wives', 170.

already seen that the church's submission to Christ leads to blessing, growth, and unity for God's people. Similarly, the wife's submission to her husband, as she seeks to honour the Lord Jesus Christ, will *ultimately* lead to divine blessing for herself and others.[61]

THE BASIS OF LOVE

Ephesians 5:22–33

Sometimes, the emphasis of this passage is entirely misplaced, and it is read as if its essence was the subordination of wife to husband. The single phrase, 'The husband is the head of the wife', is quoted in isolation. But the basis of the passage is not control; it is love. Paul says certain things about the love that a husband must have for his wife.

(1) It must be a *sacrificial* love. He must love her as Christ loved the Church and gave himself for the Church. It must never be a selfish love. Christ loved the Church, not that the Church might do things for him, but that he might do things for the Church. The fourth-century Church father John Chrysostom has a wonderful expansion of this passage: 'Hast thou seen the measure of obedience? Hear also the measure of love. Wouldst thou that thy wife shouldst obey thee as the Church doth Christ? Have care thyself for her as Christ for the Church. And if it be needful that thou shouldst give thy life for her, or be cut to pieces a thousand times, or endure anything whatever, refuse it not ... He brought the Church to his feet by his great care, not by threats nor fear nor any such thing; so do thou conduct thyself

61 Peter Thomas O'Brien, *The Letter to the Ephesians*, The Pillar New Testament Commentary (Grand Rapids, MI: W.B. Eerdmans Publishing Co., 1999), 415–418.

towards thy wife.'

The husband is head of the wife—true, Paul said that; but he also said that the husband must love the wife as Christ loved the Church, with a love which never exercises a tyranny of control but which is ready to make any sacrifice for her good.

(2) It must be a *purifying* love. Christ cleansed and consecrated the Church by the washing with water on the day when each member of the Church made a personal confession of faith. It may well be that Paul has in mind a Greek custom. One of the Greek marriage customs was that, before the bride was taken to her marriage, she was bathed in the water of a stream sacred to some god or goddess. In Athens, for instance, the bride was bathed in the waters of the Callirhoe, which was sacred to the goddess Athene. It is of baptism that Paul is thinking. By the washing of baptism and by the confession of faith, Christ sought to make for himself a Church, cleansed and consecrated, until there was neither soiling spot nor disfiguring wrinkle upon it. Any love which drags a person down is false. Any love which coarsens instead of refining the character, which necessitates deceit, which weakens the moral strength, is not love. Real love is the great purifier of life.

(3) It must be a *caring* love. A man must love his wife as he loves his own body. Real love loves not to extract service, nor to ensure that its own physical comfort is attended to; it cherishes the one it loves. There is something very wrong when a man regards his wife, consciously or unconsciously, as simply the one who cooks his meals and washes his clothes and cleans his house and brings up his children.

(4) It is an *unbreakable* love. For the sake of this love, a man leaves father and mother and is joined to his wife. They become one flesh. He is as united to her as the members of the body are united to each other, and

> would no more think of separating from her than of tearing his own body apart. Here indeed was an ideal in an age when men and women changed partners with as little thought as they changed clothes.
>
> (5) The whole relationship is *in the Lord*. In the Christian home, Jesus is an always-remembered, though an unseen, guest. In Christian marriage, there are not two partners, but three—and the third is Christ.[62]

The wife should feel and know that the husband is primarily concerned with her best interest, and will always consider her views, evidencing that he values her voice in all matters. He will make sure that he listens to her and if her view is the correct view, he will wisely follow that course. A husband will demonstrate and express his love and respect for his wife when he carries out his Godly assigned position as the head of the family. (John 13:34) The husband might be imperfect and fallible, but if he follows in the example of Jesus Christ, he will have a wife that loves and respects him as well.

[62] William Barclay, *The Letters to the Galatians and Ephesians*, The New Daily Study Bible (Louisville, KY; London: Westminster John Knox Press, 2002), 200–201.

WIVES 9 How to Stop Arguing

Does it seem like you and your wife end up in one argument after another? Do you feel like you are walking on eggshells or through a minefield in which any step could cause the spouse to explode?

If this is the case, do not worry because change is possible. You and your husband can make improvements in the way you communicate. However, you and your mate need to discover why arguments keep coming up.

Misunderstandings

Is there a failure to understand or interpret something correctly at times, which leads to a minor disagreement or dispute? Are there times when you say something, and you know what you meant, but the husband reads another meaning into it. Are there times when you, the wife, say you told your husband something that he was supposed to remember, but he does not even remember you telling him?

Differences

There was a couple dating through long distance chat on Facebook. She was from Chile, and he was from America. She spoke Spanish and very little English. He spoke English and next to no Spanish. The cultural difference between two countries over 7,000 miles (11265 Kilometers) removed was a factor as well. Even two people from the same country and even the same city will face differences as to their worldviews. In this case, it is easy to misunderstand based on small or great differences in one's views, culture,[63] languages, and the like.

---

[63] **Culture** is defined as a set of values, practices, traditions or beliefs a group shares, whether due to age, race or ethnicity, religion or gender.

Bad Examples

Some people's parents argued every day about what seemed like things that were not important or significant. It baffled you as a child at how they argued over the same things year after year, day after day. In these arguments, as things escalated, your parents might have said many disrespectful things to each other. One couple argued every day, almost like clockwork, would say the most heinous things to each other. After a few hours of not speaking to one another, the next thing in the process was a couple of hours of I love you.

Beneath the Surface

Many times the argument is not even really about what got it started. There is something else beneath the surface, which ignites and fuels an argument. Maybe, you are deep in an argument as to why you are always late! It is not so much about your punctuality as it is your spouse feels as though she is being taken for granted or treated thoughtlessly in a number of things.

Regardless of the cause, frequent arguments have a major impact on a marriage. Not only will it eventually cause the love for each other to cool down, so you grow apart, it will cause health damages as well. Thus, the question, how can you stop arguing?

Steps to fewer Arguments

Why do I say fewer arguments? Before we list what we can do, it is best that we revisit just what our circumstances are as imperfect humans. If a human knows that, they suffer from turrets syndrome, it is no surprise to them or their spouse that they compulsively utter obscenities. Certainly, a wife of a husband or a husband of a wife would not be as troubled by their spouse who utters obscenities because of suffering from turrets syndrome. Therefore, the same married couple should have an understanding of their spouse suffering from inherited sin, imperfections, and human weaknesses, so as to make allowances for falling short. Just how bad is it?

There are four factors to our stress and difficult times **(1)** We are imperfect and live in an imperfect world, compounded by the fact that God's Word says we are mentally bent and lean toward doing bad. We read, "When the LORD saw that the wickedness of man on the earth was great and that the whole bent of his thinking was never anything but evil, the LORD regretted that he had ever made man on the earth." (Gen. 6:5, AT) **(2)** We have a wicked spirit creature, Satan the Devil, who is misleading the entire world of humankind. We read, "Be sober-minded;[64] be watchful. Your adversary, the devil, prowls around like a roaring lion, seeking someone to devour." (1 Pet. 5:8) **(3)** We live in a world that caters to the imperfect flesh. We read, "For all that is in the world, the lust of the flesh and the lust of the eyes and the boastful pride of life, is not from the Father, but is from the world. The world is passing away, and its lusts; but the one who does the will of God remains forever." (1 John 2:16-17) **(4)** We are unable to understand our inner person, which the Bible informs us is wicked: "The heart is deceitful above all things and desperately sick; who can understand it?" The apostle Paul tells us, "just as sin came into the world through one man, and death through sin, and so death spread to all men because all sinned." There is only one major factor in all four parts that will have an effect on the other two, **you.**—Jeremiah 17:9; Romans 5:12.

Yes, at times, we create our own stress. Because **(1)** we do not understand our true imperfection, and our

---

[64] **Sober Minded**: (Gr. *nepho*) This denotes being sound in mind, to be in control of one's thought processes and thus not be in danger of irrational thinking, 'to be sober-minded, to be well composed in mind.'—1 Thessalonians 5:6, 8; 2 Timothy 4:5; 1 Peter 1:13; 4:7; 5:8

imperfection is easily misled by point number **(2)**, Satan. Moreover, we are easily enticed by point numbers **(3-4)**, the world and its desires, as well as our heart. We read, "But each one is tempted when he is carried away and enticed by his own desire.[65] Then the desire when it has conceived gives birth to sin, and sin when it is fully grown brings forth death." (Jam. 1:14-15, ESV) Only by an active faith in Christ, and a true understanding of our imperfection, can we hope to function in an imperfect world, defeat Satan, gain control over our imperfect flesh, allow God to read our heart and help us **not** to fall victim to our own desires of the eyes? Moreover, many times, it is our imperfect perception of an incident that angers us, not necessarily the spouse.

What Can You Do

If you are serious, you will want to identify the true issue that lies beneath the argument. Just as a noise in a car is not the real problem, it is whatever is lying behind that noise, so too, the argument itself is not the problem. When you and your spouse are getting along, try the following.

Pull out those same two tablets, so that you and your spouse can write down what you believe a recent argument was about. The husband may write, "you were out all day with your friends and **never** called so I would know where you were." Then, the wife writes, "You are **always** angry because I spend time with my friends."

First, we note the absolute thinking errors. **Absolute thinking** is the tendency to think in concrete, black and white terms. "I am absolutely delighted" or "I am absolutely devastated." A cognitive error in which events are interpreted in total or **absolute** ways; thus failure at

---

[65] Or "own *lust*"

a particular task might lead to the thought "I cannot do anything right."

Second, consider just how serious the so-called offense was. Is this one of those things that we make allowances for, concerning our spouse because of human imperfection? We have to realize that human imperfection will affect the both of us. In many cases, just agree to disagree. Wise King Solomon said, "Whoever covers an offense seeks love, but he who repeats a matter separates close friends." (Prov. 17:9) Max Anders writes, "When someone has committed an **offense** against you or some third party, you have two options available: cover it over by a discreet silence or publicize it through gossip and complaint. Your choice affects more than just yourself. Covering the offense **promotes love** by maintaining an atmosphere of trust; the person who **repeats the matter** stirs up suspicion, even among **close friends**."[66]

If the matter was insignificant, just apologize, and the other accepts the apology. Then, never bring it up again.

Colossians 3:13-14 Updated American Standard Version (UASV)

[13] putting up with one another and forgiving one another. If anyone should have a complaint against another, forgiving each other; as the Lord has forgiven you, so you also must forgive. [14] And above all these things put on love, which is a perfect bond of union.

On the other hand, if it is a significant wrong, there is another step in this process.

---

[66] Anders, Max. Holman Old Testament Commentary - Proverbs (p. 222). B&H Publishing. Kindle Edition.

On your tablet, write down what you were feeling during the argument. The husband writes, "I felt as though your friends were more important than me." While the wife writes, I felt like I was being treated like a child and you were my father, whom I had to check in every two hours."

Now, you hand your tablet to your husband and take his, reading each other's comments. Now, take note of the issue beneath the surface of the argument for each other. Without arguing more, talk about how you felt and what you could (not what the other could) have done differently. Solomon wrote, "A fool gives full vent to his spirit, but a wise man quietly holds it back." (Prov. 29:11) Anders writes, "One of the characteristics of a **fool** is his inability to hold back his anger (literally, his spirit). A **wise man**, on the other hand, keeps his temper **under control**, even in a confrontation. The Hebrew for keeping oneself under control is literally "to calm it back"; the same word is used in Psalms 65:7 and 89:9 to describe the stilling of a storm. What a perfect picture of a godly response when we are tempted to blow up!"[67]

Now, take a moment to discuss what you have learned throughout this process. How will it help you to decrease the number of arguments? What was it that each of you truly needs during your dispute, which would have claimed the emotional responses? Was it understanding?

Proverbs 17:9 Updated American Standard Version (UASV)

[9] Whoever covers a transgression seeks love,
    but he who repeats a matter separates close friends.

---

[67] Anders, Max. Holman Old Testament Commentary - Proverbs (p. 198). B&H Publishing. Kindle Edition.

WIVES 10 How to Avoid Hurtful Words

Some spouses enter into a conflict with argumentative tones, and before you know, a flood of hurtful criticism is being hurled at each other. If this grows without finding a way to decrease, it will then become your normal way of communicating with each other. If this is the way of your marriage, you can stop this form of communication. If it has not grown into this pattern of normalcy, you can cut it off at the roots, so that it does not become a norm.

Why Loving People Say Hurtful Words

It should be noted that the godly qualities that our Creator has given us are in every one of us, even in our imperfection. However, we do have another inner desire that wars against our desires to follow the qualities that God has instilled in us. Because of our imperfection, again, we are mentally bent toward evil. (Gen. 6:5; 8:21; Ps. 51:5, AT) Moreover, our heart (inner person, the seat of motivation) 'is deceitful above all things, and desperately sick; which we cannot understand.' (Jer. 17:9) Therefore, if we are going to maintain and develop the quality of putting other people's needs, interests, or wishes before our own, we must cultivate our selfless side. This is especially true within the family because if one person is a selfish person, it will be a life of pain and suffering for everyone else. The reality is, it was the selfishness of Satan, Adam, and Eve that has humankind living in imperfection, pain, suffering, old age, and death. Sadly, every argument between family and friends, every conflict between leaders, every war between nations, every dispute between employer and employee, and every crime is the result of selfishness. Our concern with our own interests, needs, and wishes while ignoring those

91

of others will ruin our life and any relationship we might ever hope to have.

What motivates us to be selfless? It is another human quality, empathy, the ability to identify with and understand somebody else's feelings or difficulties. When we do something for another, like pay for a military person's meal at a restaurant, we are empathizing with what he gave up, so we have the freedom we have. This brings us to another quality, gratitude, i.e., being thankful for what others have done. Imagine, the traffic is moving slowly, and we are laying on our horn because we are in a hurry. Soon, we see several ambulances ahead. As we drive by a car wreck, we see a teenage girl being zipped up in a black body bag. Suddenly, our heart is beating heavily; we feel the pain of that child, the pain of the mother, and our being late for a meeting is the furthest thing from our mind. If we have never pondered whether we carry out selfless acts, we might start with something small. We might focus on getting the door for people, offering better tips for service, helping someone in a small way, considering how others might feel, and seeing how we react to inconveniences. When we see how others react to our small acts of kindness, will help us to develop our selfless side further.

The apostle Paul wrote, "Let each one keep seeking, not his own good, but that of the other person." (1 Cor. 10:24) On this verse, Bible scholar David E. Garland writes, "Paul's command that one "not seek that which is one's own" leaves indefinite what they are not to seek.[2] We can fill in the blank with words such as "advantage," "interest," "good," "ends," "enjoyment," "needs." Instead of selfish things, they are to seek the interests of the other ... This "other" is not restricted to the fellow believer who might have a weak conscience, as in 8:11, but also includes the unbeliever who might offer an invitation to dinner (10:27). His concern in this section is not the effect of their behavior on other believers but its effect on nonbelievers. The overarching hermeneutical principles that govern his practical advice are these: What course of action will bring glory to God, and what course of action will be "the most effective witness to Christ?" (Ruef 1977: 103). Paul expects the Corinthians to do all things to bring glory to God (10:31) and to seek the best interests of others so that they might be saved (10:33)." (Garland 2003, p. 489)

As was stated in the last chapter, some husbands and wives were raised in homes where hurtful words were common among the parents, among the children to the parents, and overhearing the parents talk badly about others. It can be a learned behavior, which can simply be unlearned.

Moreover, we have an entertainment industry today that flourishes with harmful words, the more there are, the bigger the box office sales. Comedians today say the most hurtful things about husbands and wives, as well as children.

In some cultures around the world, men view women as less of a person and feel that real men must dominate their women. In these cultures, if a woman offers her thoughts on something to the male, it is viewed as challenging the husband, and he looks weak to the other men. In such a culture, family arguments are viewed as being between enemies, not husbands and wives, using hurtful words.

Hurtful words unchecked will eventually lead to a divorce, not to mention the health problem that comes from heated exchanges. Some husbands and wives would say that hurtful words do more damage to the soul that fists do to the body because the body heals, the hurt soul lingers for years to come.

What can you do if hurtful words have already begun to encroach on your relationship with your wife?

What you Can Do

EMPATHY is the understanding of another's feelings: the ability to identify with and understand somebody else's feelings or difficulties. Try not to focus on your pain but imagine what your spouse must be feeling. Walk through arguments that you have had and think of the hurtful words that you have used. Now, ponder how the words must have impacted him. Do not consider what was said or what the argument was about, just the hurtful words that you used and how they must have made your husband feel.

After that, now consider your husband's hurtful words **but make allowances** for your husband's words. Say things to yourself like, maybe he had a past girlfriend that verbally, mentally and emotionally abused him. Does it seem like his words coming from that perspective? Can you understand his reaction is not entirely about you? While it is true that no person should suffer the consequences of another person's past action, it is also true that the husband's actions may be a product of abuse too.

Proverbs 15:1 Updated American Standard Version (UASV)

15 A gentle answer turns away wrath,
   but a painful[68] word stirs up anger.

Max Anders writes, "How can we handle an angry person? Our instinctive response is to come back with a **harsh**, hurtful retort, a tactic that just escalates the level of rage. The other option is a **gentle**, soft **answer**. The wise person can avoid needless quarrels by defusing a

---

[68] I.e. *harsh*

tense situation. Such tact requires forethought, patience, self-control, and kindness."[69]

If your life has been the result of parents, who set a bad example with their hard words, you can relearn respect by observing other couples that respect each other. Watch how they interact with each other. The apostle Paul wrote, "Brothers, join in imitating me, and observe those who walk according to the example you have in us." (Phil. 3:17) "Paul's example was Christ. He then lived out the Christ model as he ran the race. He appealed to his readers to follow his example. Some already followed that example, so they, too, serve as models for the Philippians. They had a choice. They could model their lives after those advocating falsehood and fail to win the prize, or they could model their lives after Christ."[70] Some couples have mastered the Christ model in their relationship; you can imitate their fine example as well.

Hurtful words come from the mind, not the heart or the mouth. The heart and the mouth are just vehicles that carry our thoughts to fruition. It is your perception of things that contribute (not cause) to anger that leads to hurtful words. If you can change your perception, i.e., your way of thinking, you can change how you feel, which will change how you act.

Overcoming Should Statements

We need to come to the realization that nothing or no one is responsible for our anger issues. It is we and we alone. It is common by those that suffer from unrighteous anger to believe; it is the conditions, which cause the

---

[69] Anders, Max. Holman Old Testament Commentary - Proverbs (p. 211). B&H Publishing. Kindle Edition.

[70] Max Anders, *Galatians-Colossians*, vol. 8, Holman New Testament Commentary (Nashville, TN: Broadman & Holman Publishers, 1999), 246.

outbursts. The truth is nothing can cause us to get angry. However, the events or situations can contribute to our getting angry if we feed them with irrational thinking. When an unpleasant situation falls upon us, we can feel the physical effects of a racing heart, tension in our muscles, the grinding of our teeth, and so on. These physical signs mean that we are dialoguing with ourselves either consciously or subconsciously. Yes, these thoughts can be present in the mind without our awareness of it. It is the physical signs that must wake us up to hidden thoughts.

If you are aware of what you are thinking, because you are saying it aloud, even if it is mumbling under your breath, or you have hidden comments that you are unaware of, you have signs to let you know. You need to be the one to reverse course. You must ask yourself, "What am I saying." Get a grasp of the thoughts that are racing through your mind. Maybe the events are with your spouse. First, we set ourselves up for failure, because the dating stage of a relationship is unrealistic. During this stage, both parties do their best to present nothing but the best side of themselves. After the honeymoon, a few months down the road, both begin to get comfortable and let down and show they flawed qualities. It could be a rude awakening, even more so if either of the spouses felt that the marriage was going to be some perfect storybook life, with a happy ending.

If he says she should be like this, or he should be like that, this is another unrealistic aspect. We will get angry if we are caught up in the syndrome of *should*. A Christian marriage should be this way. Life should be like this, or like that. We must realize that we can even do this with ourselves as well. "I should do this, or I should do that." When someone or we do not live up to our expectation, this can contribute to frustration. "I should have been paying closer attention." "He should have been more

96

considerate." Generally, we are making these should statement before we are even aware all of the facts.

This *should* syndrome will affect our lives far more than we may ever imagine, contributing to a life of tumult. When we go around setting standards of perfection for others, and ourselves (meaning mistake free), when humankind is imperfect, we are just setting ourselves up for a life of disappointment. We are going to fall short of our own standards that we have set, every day, as an imperfect person. Everyone is going to fall short of our standard setting of what we believe he or she should be like. We expect them to act a certain way in certain circumstances. We expect them to talk a certain way, drive a certain way, react a certain way, live a certain way, believe a certain way, and so on.

When we do not live up to our *should* standards of being mistake free, falling short daily, our statements of "I *should*" are going to contribute to an intense dislike of self, unworthiness and embarrassment, faultfinding, and frustration. When the rest of humanity does not live up to our *should* standards of them, namely being mistake free, we will become hostile toward them, have a self-righteous attitude that they should have done better. Imagine, we are only addressing one word, which possesses so much power, and by changing it, we can free ourselves of constant let downs.

Christians, sad to say, are more susceptible to these *should* statements. Because we are involved in a biblical worldview that revolves around the moral values of God, we tend to begin thinking more of ourselves than we ought to, when we become more successful in our spiritual lives. When we take a pause to notice our should statements, we will see that the vast majority revolve around morality, standards of conduct that are generally accepted as right or wrong. "He should have done a better job in mowing the lawn because I pay him more than enough!" The rational side of that is that there are no rules that the lawn company has to go above the standards for us; he need not take extra pride in his work, just because we think he should. It is perfectly fine to do a standard job, as long as it is not substandard. Another should stamen might be, "He should have thought to call if he knew he was going to be late because it is the decent thing to do!" He probably feels that he should have remembered as well, but he is imperfect, and so is his memory, especially when he is deeply involved in his job.

Our should statements assume that we are entitled to error free people, including ourselves. If we have been "wronged" because of human imperfection, make allowances, forgive them as God forgives us every day. If we have been wronged because of substandard behavior, take care of it in a rational manner. If we deal with it through anger, we will not get the desired outcome. Rather we will only end up with a defensive person, be it a family member, friend, or another, who may not have had bad intentions to start with, but now he is being pushed into a corner. Think of the folly of this statement, "I was nice to the people at that table, being a good waitress; they should have given me a tip." We cannot be the over someone else's free will, their right to live life the way they believe to be correct. As much as we may desire that they live by our standards, our wanting it will not bring it about.

In fact, if we react inappropriately to what we believe they should or should not do, it will only create bitterness in our stomach, and distance them from us. We certainly detest the idea of anyone taking control of the way we do things, and this is the case with all free-willed people. Once we realize that there is no such thing as absolute fairness among imperfect humanity, as it is relative to the one carrying out the actions. What we see as fair biblically, the world sees as unfair. There is absolute fairness with God, as well as his Word the Bible, but at present, the world of mankind alienated from God do not live by that fairness.

When talking to your spouse, do not say "you did" but rather "I feel" to express your concerns of how things affected you. For example, "**I feel** hurt when you do so many things with letting me know. I worry about you." The other poor choice of hurtful words would be, "That is **just like you, you are** always making plans without checking with me first. Again, Paul said, "Let your speech always be gracious, seasoned with salt, so that you may know how you ought to answer each person."– Colossians 4:6.

Ephesians 4:31-32 Updated American Standard Version (UASV)

[31] Let all bitterness and wrath and anger and clamor and **abusive words** be put away from you, along with all malice. [32] Be kind to one another, tender-hearted, forgiving each other, just as God in Christ also has forgiven you.[71]

Abusive Words: (Gr. *blasphēmia*) This is referring to reviling, malicious talk, abusive words, slander (Matt. 15:19); blasphemy, the content of defamation or slander (Lu 5:21). This is abusive words that are spoken in anger, which could be intentionally or unintentionally hurting another, as well as damaging their reputation.

---

[71] Two early mss read *us*

WIVES 11 How to Discuss Problems

At times, when you and your wife are discussing family problems, it starts nice enough but ends with the two of your father remove than when you began. Of course, any learned behavior can be unlearned. Let us consider. As was mentioned earlier, men and women have different ways that they communicate.

As was mention, men are more likely to want to offer quick fixes to the problem, while wives want to talk about the problem in relation to their feelings. Women generally would like to discuss the problem before looking for a solution. They are comforted by being able to express their feelings and know that you, the husband understand them. In some cases, the wife will feel that the talking about the problem is the solution itself. For the woman, she can talk about the problem in minutes and then she is completely over it, while the man tends to ponder what just happened. He might spend the rest of the day thinking nothing got resolved. The husband was not looking for feelings but rather what is the root of the problem and how can we deal with that. He wants to discuss solutions. The fixing of the problem makes the husband feel like progress has been made. This solution-finding mission for the husband is his way of showing the wife he cares and that she can rely on him. He is bewildered at the idea of talking about a problem without talking about the root and looking for a solution.

However, both the husband and wife are right. It takes both talking about the problem and feelings, as well as looking for the root and solving it. The wife needs to express her feeling about the problem, how it impacts her and the husband needs to communicate that he understands her feelings. Then, it is time to move to the root of the problem, followed by solutions. However, you have to be a good listener first. Then the wife needs to be patient as you get your side of things taken care of, so the both of you feel fulfilled.

How to Comfort Your Distressed Husband with Words

Active Listening

Proverbs 20:5 Updated American Standard Version (UASV)

⁵ Counsel in a man's heart is like deep water,
    but a man of understanding draws it out.

Proverbs 18:13 Updated American Standard Version (UASV)

¹³ If one gives an answer before he hears,
    it is his folly and shame.

We need to be able to hear the words that are spoken, as well as the way that it is said, the tone, the body language, so at to get the sense of what is being meant. A common complaint of wives to husbands is that they passively listen to them, blocking out much of what they do not want to hear, because they are opposed, or are not interested in what she is saying. Sadly, we tend to be less appreciative of those who are closest to us than total strangers. Active listening is a form of listening that results in both the speaker and listener having a full understanding of what is meant. There are five points to keep in mind:

(1) Pay close attention to what is being said; listen for the ideas behind the words. Do not just hear, but also feel the words. Let the speaker know that you are listening, by leaning forward a little, looking at him, not staring, but having periodic eye contact.

(2) Look at facial expression, the tone of the voice, the inflection of the voice, the mood and body language. You want to get at the feelings behind the words. People generally do not say all that is on their mind or convey their true feelings at times, so you have to pay close attention to the non-verbal.

(3) Turn off your internal thinking as much as possible. In other words, do not be thinking of how to respond to certain points while he is still talking, because you are going to miss the whole of what he has said.

(4) Let the speaker know **you are paying attention** by nodding from time to time, as well as acknowledging with verbal gestures.

(5) Reiterate is not a common word, but it means to repeat what you think the person meant by what they said, but in your own words, to see if you understood correctly. So, you mean … right?'

(6) The person you are speaking with will **acknowledge either you are correct, or he will correct you**, and will restate what they meant, and likely in a more comprehensive way since you misunderstood.

(7) When they have explained their message again, you must **repeat your reiteration**.

Be Empathetic

1 Peter 3:8 Updated American Standard Version (UASV)

[8] Finally, all of you, have like-minded, sympathy, brotherly love, tender hearted, and humble-minded;

Romans 12:15 Updated American Standard Version (UASV)

15 Rejoice with those who rejoice, and weep with those who weep.

One of the ways to deal with a challenge is to have empathy. You in your heart must place yourself in their circumstances, getting their mindset. Just because a person comes across abrasively at times, this does not mean that you let them go. There may very well be a reason as to why they are not open to the conversation. This is where insightful, thought-provoking questions, can get at the significant part that has closed them down.

By employing active listening, allowing them to vent, you will understand whatever issues you need to overcome. You might ask, 'tell me, what has you to the point where you are unable to talk this.' This will let them know that you are open to listening. While they are expressing themselves, do not be tempted to resolve their issue, just listen as they fully explain. First, make sure you respond in a calm voice. Then reiterate what they said in a summary point, which will let them know you were listening, and it helps you to know you understand what it is. In the end, you may not agree, but you can empathetically understand in some way.

Be Patient

Psalm 103:14 Updated American Standard Version (UASV)

14 For he [God] himself knows our formation;
   he remembers that we are dust.

Many times, one has to realize that not every conversation is going to reach a resolution. Therefore, one needs to be patient, and wait for a better time, as it will come up again. Another part of patience is being able to overlook the things the sufferer may say that is hurtful. Recognize that it is the illness speaking, and make allowances accordingly.

Use Your Words Wisely

Proverbs 25:11 Contemporary English Version (CEV)

¹¹ The right word
at the right time
is like precious gold
set in silver.

Proverbs 15:23 Updated American Standard Version (UASV)

²³ A man has joy in the answer of his mouth,
and a word in season, how good it is!

Use your words to strengthen the depressed one, help him or her to see their good qualities. Be specific in your praises. Let them know that the problems that you face together, the troubles of the past, and time when you both have fallen short are not reflective of the good person he or she is.

WIVES 12 How to Solve Problems In Your Marriage

Some husbands struggle to control their anger. Then, the husband and wife might have disagreements about different family situations. Then, there is a breakdown in the communication. As this author keeps reminding the reader, you need to keep reminding yourselves; no marriage will ever be perfect. This is no fairy tale where everything works out just fine all the time. However, it will have a happy ending.

Proverbs 18:19 Updated American Standard Version (UASV)

[19] A brother offended is more unyielding than a fortified city,
   and there are disputes like the bars of a fortress.

In looking at the historical setting of this verse, Max Anders tells us, "Conquering an opposing army in the open field was always easier than gaining a fortified city. In fact, one reason Joshua asked God to lengthen the day during the battle at Gibeon was to enable him to destroy the enemy armies before they could reach the safety of their home cities (Josh. 10:11). An invading army could try to climb the walls, demolish the walls or gates with a battering ram, build a ramp to the top, or dig tunnels underneath. If such efforts failed, the enemy would simply surround the city and wait for water and food supplies to run out. This, however, could take years. The Assyrians besieged Samaria for three years (2 Kgs. 17:5), and the Babylonians camped around Jerusalem for eighteen months (Jer. 52:4)."[72]

---

[72] Anders, Max. Holman Old Testament Commentary - Proverbs (p. 238). B&H Publishing. Kindle Edition.

This principle behind proverb is related to the marriage in that, over time, if you do not resolve the problems of marriage, these problems might be "like the bars of a fortress," which block communication altogether. Therefore, you need to open the door of effective communication

What It Takes for Effective Communication

Matthew 11:28-30 Updated American Standard Version (UASV)

Jesus' Yoke Is Refreshing

28 "Come to me, all you who are laboring and loaded down, and I will give you rest. 29 Take my yoke upon you and learn from me, for I am **gentle** and **lowly in heart**, and you will find rest for your souls. 30 For my yoke is easy,73 and my burden is light."

Yes, if we are going to be an effective communicator, we must learn from Jesus. What do we learn from Jesus? First, Jesus is "gentle," which is the English for the Greek word *praus* that is found "three times in Matthew and once in 1 Peter ... means 'gentle, humble, considerate, meek in the older favorable sense' (BAGD)."74 In what sense was Jesus, "lowly in heart"?75

---

73 I.e. *easy to bear*

74 Leon Morris, The Gospel According to Matthew, The Pillar New Testament Commentary (Grand Rapids, MI; Leicester, England: W.B. Eerdmans; Inter-Varsity Press, 1992).

75 The heart ([kardia]) is the core and center of man's being, the mainspring of dispositions as well as of feelings and thoughts. It is the very hub of the wheel of man's existence, the center from which all the spokes radiate (Prov. 4:23; cf. 1 Sam. 16:7). All of this also applies to Christ's human nature.—William Hendriksen and Simon J. Kistemaker, vol. 9, Exposition of the Gospel According to Matthew, New Testament Commentary (Grand Rapids: Baker Book House, 1953-2001).

With his knowledge and understanding, as the Son of God, he could have taught in Jewish schools, having some of the greatest Jewish minds as his students. He could have taught the Jewish teachers themselves if he so desired.

However, Jesus chose to teach the lowliest of the Jewish world, from the seaside, fishermen. He lived and taught among the poor and the low in social position. It is a privilege to pattern ourselves after such a teacher as he was. This humility and lowliness of heart qualified him as the greatest teacher ever so it will qualify us, as he teaches us, to be teachers of others. When we are lowly in heart, following in the footsteps of Jesus, we too will refresh our wife. A husband who is gentle, humble, considerate, meek, will bring comfort to his wife. The wife with a receptive heart will find you refreshing, respecting you in your conversations all the more.

In Acts 20:19, it says that the Apostle Paul served the Lord "with all humility," with "humble-mindedness" or "humility of mind." The Greek (*tapeinophrosune*) literally reads "lowliness of mind."[76] It is derived from the words *tapeinos*, which means to "make low," "lowly, "humble" and *phren*, "the mind." Paul told the Philippians that they were to "do nothing from selfish ambition or conceit, but in humility **["lowliness of mind"]** count others more significant than yourselves." (Phil. 2:3-4) Paul also told the Corinthians, "Let no one seek his own good but the good of the other." (1 Cor. 10:24) This quality of "lowliness of mind" will stop you from assuming a superior attitude or tone when you speak to your wife.

---

[76] W. E. Vine, Merrill F. Unger and William White, Jr., vol. 2, Vine's Complete Expository Dictionary of Old and New Testament Words, 314 (Nashville, TN: T. Nelson, 1996).

Additionally, if you want to be effective in your communication, one must follow Paul's counsel found at Colossians 4:6,

Colossians 4:6 Updated American Standard Version (UASV)

[6] Let your speech always be gracious, seasoned with salt, so that you may know how you ought to answer each person.

Certainly, patience and tact, which is skillfully expressing yourself when your wife's feelings are involved, are two qualities that establish effective communication. When you communicate with your wife, your words must be in good taste. Good speech will keep lines of communication open, but unwise, foolish, and careless comments will close those lines of communication.

If you are prepared to talk to your wife you will not be anxious but will be relaxed, which will have a calming effect on your wife, too. However, allow your wife to do most of the talking, to get at the heart of their thinking and feelings. You can never understand your wife's thinking because if you do not know what is going through her mind. For example, your wife could make a comment, and you could choose a phrase and give several minutes of feedback, which proves to be irrelevant to what she meant. It would have been better to ask, "What do you mean by ...?" Once she explains herself, then you can offer your thoughts.

Loving Communication

The characteristics of being gentle, humble, considerate, meek, modest, lowliness of mind, tactfulness and patience make the qualities of a good communicator. When you also have selfless love, you will become a great communicator.

Matthew 9:36 Updated American Standard Version (UASV)

³⁶ When he saw the crowds, he had compassion for them, because they were **harassed** and **scattered**, like sheep without a shepherd.

Mark 6:34 Updated American Standard Version (UASV)

³⁴ When he went ashore he saw a great crowd, and he had compassion on them, because they were like sheep without a shepherd. And he began to teach them many things.

"**Harassed** is from a verb meaning to trouble, distress. **Scattered** is from a verb meaning to throw down. The past tense used here implies the thoroughness of their oppression and its persistent effect on the people. These people were completely and perpetually discouraged."[77] The Jewish religious leaders of Jesus' day did next to nothing in offering enough to make common people feel pleased or content in their spiritual hunger. Rather, they made their lives even more burdensome with all of their rules and regulations that they tacked on to the Mosaic Law. (Matt. 12:1, 2; 15:1-9; 23:4, 23) The religious leaders revealed their true heart condition when they said about those listening to Jesus, "this crowd who does not know the law is accursed!" (John 7:49) Jesus' selfless love moved him to "find rest for their souls," getting on the road to life. Today, you as the loving husband have the mind of Christ that is filled with love as well, and you must offer love to your wife in a selfless way, too.

---

[77] Stuart K. Weber, vol. 1, Matthew, Holman New Testament Commentary, 130 (Nashville, TN: Broadman & Holman Publishers, 2000).

1 Thessalonians 2:7-8 Updated American Standard Version (UASV)

⁷ But we became gentle⁷⁸ in the midst of you, as a nursing mother tenderly care for⁷⁹ her own children. ⁸ So, being affectionately desirous of you, we were well-pleased to impart to you not only the gospel of God but also our own souls,⁸⁰ because you became beloved to us.

2:7. Instead, Paul and Silas chose to be **gentle**. There is no tenderness quite like a mother's, and Paul dared to identify with maternal love and care. Greek writers used the term *gentleness* to describe those who dealt patiently and with a mild manner toward those who were difficult—obstinate children, unmanageable students, those who had not reached maturity and were experiencing the inconsistencies and struggles of development. Whatever difficulties the Thessalonians may have presented, Paul and Silas recognized that these new Christians were not yet "grown up." So rather than dealing with these people in an authoritarian manner, they chose to be patient—like a mother.

It is a great lesson for the church today, because we have not always been patient with new or young believers. Sometimes we have cut a mold and demanded that they fit it—now. Instead of this approach, we need to see each individual's need for help and encouragement as he or she struggles to conform to the image of Christ.

2:8. Here is a classic understanding of biblical love. To Paul, love is always a verb, it is doing. Feelings may accompany love, but they do not define it. Instead, the commitment of acting in the best interest of another

---

⁷⁸ Some MSS read *babes*

⁷⁹ Or *cherishes*

⁸⁰ Or *lives*

opens the way for feelings: **We loved you so much that we were delighted to share ... our lives**.

It is easier to teach theology than to love, easier to share lists than time. Paul gave not only the message of the gospel, but the example of it as well. He spent time. He shared joys and headaches. Parents and teachers, coaches and mentors, pastors and leaders know what it means to give part of their heart away to others. Love is not just a job. It is a way of life.

But note that Paul did *share* the gospel of God. He was balanced. He gave his life and love. He gave content as well. It is not enough to visit people in the hospital or prison, or to show compassion to the poor or those new in the faith. Somewhere, carefully and candidly, they must also hear the truth of the cross and what it means to trust and follow Christ.

Arguing whether the church should meet people's physical needs or whether it should limit itself to preaching the gospel is like debating which wing of an airplane is more important. Both are essential![81]

The Apostle Paul started numerous congregations, one right after the other, from Antioch of Syria, throughout Asia, into Macedonia, down through Greece and Achaia. The apostle Paul was like a father to thousands of Christians. What made Paul such an effective evangelist? Was it his zeal for spreading the Good News? Yes! The above says that Paul was **"affectionately desirous"** of the new Thessalonian congregation. "Here is a classic understanding of biblical love. To Paul, love is always a verb, it is doing. Feelings may accompany love, but they do not define it. Instead,

[81] Knute Larson, *I & II Thessalonians, I & II Timothy, Titus, Philemon*, vol. 9, Holman New Testament Commentary (Nashville, TN: Broadman & Holman Publishers, 2000), 23–24.

the commitment to acting in the best interest of [your wife] opens the way for feelings: **We loved you so much that we were delighted to share ... our lives**."[82] The love Paul had for God, and his neighbor made him a successful evangelist.

If your wife repeatedly rejects your communication, this is a sign of poor communication skills. Have you done your best to be an effective communicator with your wife, when any opportunity presents itself? If you answered yes, and she still has felt troubled or hurt during your communication times, you might want to consider the qualities of Jesus and Paul in the above text. Do an isolated study of what those words mean. Then, start focusing on one at a time, seeing how you can use it in your daily life.

Four Steps to Solving Problems

(1) Do not just start talking about a major problem. Find a good day and time to discuss the issue. This will allow both of you to ponder your approach. You might want to set a regular time each week that is set aside to discuss family problems. Try to find that day and time where both are less stressed.

(2) Allow your wife to express her feeling and talk openly about the problem, while you respectfully listen. Keep in mind; you are not looking to win some battle between you and her.

(3) Then, once she has completely finished, you need to acknowledge what she has said,

---

[82] Knute Larson, vol. 9, I & II Thessalonians, I & II Timothy, Titus, Philemon, Holman New Testament Commentary, 24 (Nashville, TN: Broadman & Holman Publishers, 2000).

reiterating it, and letting her know you fully understand her feelings. Do not reuse her words when you repeat her sentiments back to her. Say it in your own words, telling her what she has said and how she feels. Never assume that you know what she means. Ask if she has said something ambiguous.

(4) Find common ground and agree on a solution. Marriage is a team, both needs to work together.

A husband and wife that fail to work together as a team will end up with a failed marriage. Then again, if you work together, there is no problem that cannot be resolved.

WIVES 13 Your Dignified Role In the Marriage

God created Adam first, then Eve. Adam had spent some time in the garden before the creation of Eve, gaining some experience in living as a new creation. During this period, God gave Adam some instruction. (Gen. 2:15-20) Being the first to be created, Adam was to take the lead in this new family arrangement. His initial role was his informing Eve about the things he had learned from God before her creation, such as the eating from the trees.

Today, the Christian congregation is the same. The apostle Paul wrote, "I do not permit a woman ... to exercise authority over a man, but to be in silence. For Adam was formed first, then Eve." (1 Tim. 2:12-13) This does not mean that the woman cannot talk in the Christian congregation. She is to be silent as in not challenging the authority of men by belittling his lead over the congregation, nor to teach the congregation. This does not mean that she cannot teach the Sunday school for the children or even a Bible study group for women. However, the primary teaching of the Christian congregation is the men's responsibility alone.[83]

The apostle Paul offers us insights into the role of men and women when he wrote, "For man is not from woman, but woman from man. For indeed man was not created for the sake of the woman, but woman for the sake of the man. This is why the woman ought to have a symbol of authority on her head, because of the angels. Nevertheless, in the Lord neither is woman separate from man nor is man separate from woman. For just as the

---

[83] Women In the Pulpit? (July 30, 2017)

https://christianpublishinghouse.co/2017/01/03/women-in-the-pulpit/

woman is from the man, so also the man is through the woman; but all things are from God."–1 Corinthians 11:8-12.

Looking back at the Law given to the Israelites rights, freedoms, and was treated with honor. They could show their ability to act on your own and make decisions without the help or advice of their husband. Proverbs 31:10-31 speaks of "An excellent wife" who with her own hands gladly makes clothes for the family. Why she even makes clothes to sell to the shop owners. (Verses 13, 21-24) She is like a sailing ship that brings food from across the sea. (Verse 14) She knows how to buy land and how to plant a vineyard. (Verse 16) She knows when to buy or sell, and she stays busy until late at night. (Verse 18) She helps the poor and the needy. She takes good care of her family and is never lazy. (Verses 20, 27) Thus, the wife was shown respect and praised in public for what she had done.–Verse 31.

The opportunity for women to make spiritual progress existed under the Mosaic Law. In Joshua 8:35, we read, "There was not a word of all that Moses had commanded that Joshua did not read aloud in front of all the congregation of Israel, **including the women** and children and the foreign residents who were living among them." In the book of Nehemiah, we read about Ezra, "So Ezra the priest brought the Law before the congregation of men, **women**, and all who could listen with understanding, on the first day of the seventh month. And he read aloud from it before the public square in front of the Water Gate, from daybreak until midday, to the men, **the women**, and all who could understand; and the people listened attentively to the book of the Law. (Neh. 8:2-3) The women under Israelite Law benefited from the reading of God's Word. The women enjoyed these reading and benefited from the wisdom the same as the men did.

Then, we move to the days of Jesus, where we find several women tending to the needs of Jesus, playing an important role in his ministry. (Lu 8:1-3) While the men treated Jesus with disdain, we find one woman that saw Jesus as so special, "a woman with an alabaster jar of costly perfumed oil approached him, and she began pouring it on his head as he was dining," anointing Jesus. (Matt. 26:6-13; John 12:1-7) It was a woman, namely, Mary Magdalene, who was the first person that Jesus appeared to after his resurrection. (Matt. 28:1-10; John 20:1-18) After Jesus had ascended back to heaven, there were 120, who met in the upper room to pray, which included "**the women** and Mary the mother of Jesus, and his brothers." (Acts 1:3-15) That means that there were women in the upper room on the day of Pentecost 33 C.E., when "they were all filled with the Holy Spirit," and many spoke in a number of different languages.–Acts 2:1-12.

It was both men and women who were among those that experienced the prophecy of Joel 2:28-29, as the Apostle Peter quoted it. He said, "I will pour out my Spirit on all flesh, and your sons and your daughters shall prophesy ... and even on my male slaves and on my female slaves I will pour out some of my Spirit in those days, and they will prophesy." (Acts 2:13-18) In the first century and into the beginning of the second century C.E., women were favored with the gifts of the Spirit.[84] They spoke in foreign languages and prophesied. Note that prophesying does not necessarily mean making

---

[84] The Holy Spirit and the Apostolic Church (July 30, 2017)
https://christianpublishinghouse.co/2017/05/26/the-holy-spirit-and-the-apostolic-church/
The Holy Spirit and the Apostles (July 30, 2017)
https://christianpublishinghouse.co/2017/05/26/the-holy-spirit-and-the-apostles/
The Holy Spirit in the First Century and Today (July 30, 2017)
https://christianpublishinghouse.co/2017/05/25/the-holy-spirit-in-the-first-century-and-today/

predictions because the Greek word (*propheteuo*) also means to proclaim the Word of God., i.e., sharing Scriptural truths. In his letter to Christians in Rome, the apostle Paul speaks affectionately of "Phoebe our sister," recommending her to them. He writes, "I commend to you our sister Phoebe, a minister of the congregation at Cenchreae." (Rom. 16:1) What does the word "minister" mean to the modern day reader?

Servant, Minister: (*diakonos*) The term can refer to one who holds the position of deacon within a Christian congregation, but the term does not necessarily mean that because the Bible uses the word *diakonos* in a broader sense, as one who waits on or attends to the needs of others. (Matt. 20:26; Rom. 16:1; Eph. 6:21; 1 Thess. 3:2) It is also used in the broad sense of those who witness to unbelievers, sharing Scriptural truths, for the purpose of converting them to the faith. (Rom. 16:1-2, 12; Phil. 4:2-3) When Paul refers to "our sister Phoebe, a minister of the congregation at Cenchreae," he is not talking about a religious leader, male or female, who presides over a congregation. Women in the first century had no position of authority within the Christian congregation as an elder (overseer) or deacon (minister, servant). They served as ministers in that "these women, [were ones] who struggled alongside [Paul] for the gospel" (Phil. 4:2-3), as well as many others to grow the Christian faith from 120 disciples in 33 C.E., to over one million disciples by 130 C.E. They were ministers in the sharing of the gospel.

A Christian sister can minister many ways today. She can be used to carry out Sunday school classes for the children, to run a Bible study for women in the congregation, to share biblical truth within her community to grow the congregation. We also have many female Christian apologists today, who defend the faith, the Bible, and God himself. Some of these have become Christian apologist authors, like Judy Salisbury.[85] Women have also played a major role in the missionary field as well.

If man and woman develop and grow their roles with the Christian congregation, as well as in the marriage, it will bring them happiness. It is when one or the other goes beyond the Word of God, trying to usurp a position that is not theirs to be had, we find conflict. Yes, the modern day feminist movement and liberal and moderate Christianity have twisted the scriptures to try to make the Bible say things that it does not. The apostle Peter tells "some things [are] hard to understand [in Paul's letters], which the untaught and unstable distort, as they do also the rest of the Scriptures, to their own destruction." (2 Pet. 3:15-16) Conservative Christian women, some with bachelor degrees, master's degrees and even doctorates in religious education do not alter the Word of God for the sake of modern feminism. The husband too does no go beyond the Scriptures, but rather he exercises his headship, not in a selfish way, but in a loving way.—Ephesians 5:25-33.

A Christian wife 'should have deep respect for her husband.' (Eph. 5:33) Max Anders writes, "**Respect** (*phobetai*) literally means "fear." It can refer, however, to the fear a person should have before God, a reverence and respect (Luke 1:50; 18:2; Acts 10:35; 1 Pet. 2:17; Rev. 14:7; 19:5). This type of reverence and regard should characterize the relationship of a wife and her husband."[86]

Peace and harmony succeed, overcome, and conquer when men and women carry out their God-

---

[85] http://tiny.cc/eemrmy

[86] Max Anders, *Galatians-Colossians*, vol. 8, Holman New Testament Commentary (Nashville, TN: Broadman & Holman Publishers, 1999), 173–174.

given roles. This results in their happiness and delight. Moreover, obeying with Scriptural requirements clothes the husband and the wife with the self-respect associated with an honored place in God's family.

WIVES 14 Dealing with Your Destructive Self-Defeating Thoughts

Prayer as Rational Self-Talk

Self-talk is what we tell ourselves in our thoughts. In fact, it is the words we tell ourselves about people, self, experiences, life, in general, God, the future, the past, the present. It is all the words that we say to ourselves all the time. Actually, if we regularly cultivate and entertain slights against us or the deeper personal affronts, it can lead to destructive depression, mood slumps, our self-worth plummeting, our body feeling sluggish, our will to accomplish even the tiniest of things is not to be realized, and our actions defeat us.

Intense negative thinking will always lead to at least a minor depressive episode or simple, painful emotion. Our thoughts based on a good mood will be entirely different from those based on our being upset. Negative thoughts that flood our mind are the actual contributors of our self-defeating emotions. These very thoughts are what keep us sluggish and contribute to our feeling frustrated, angry, or worthless. Therefore, this thinking is the key to your relief.

Every time we feel down about something, we need to attempt to locate the corresponding negative thought we had that led to this feeling down. It is these thoughts that have created our feelings of frustration, anger, or low self-worth. By learning to offset them and replace them with rational thoughts, we can actually change our mood. Remember the thoughts that move through our mind, with no effort; this is the easiest course to follow. It is so subconscious that they even go unnoticed.

The centerpiece of it all is the mind. Our moods, behaviors and body responses result from the way we view things. It is a proven fact that we cannot experience any event in any way, shape, or form unless we have processed it with our mind first. No event can depress us; it is our perception of that event that will depress us. If we are only sad over an event, our thoughts will be rational, but if we are depressed wrathful, or anxious about an event, our thinking will be bent and irrational, distorted and utterly wrong.

It may be difficult for each of us to wrap our mind around it, but we are superb at telling ourselves outright lies and half-truths, repeatedly throughout each day. In fact, some of us are so good at it that it has become our reality and led to annoyance, stress, irritation, anger, even depression, and anxiety. This section should be a beginning in helping us to start identifying these lies and half-truths.

Lies about Self

- I am dumb

- I am unattractive

- No one really likes me

- I have no talent

- I am miserable

- This always happens to me

- This is the story of my life

- Life is never going to change

- I am so lonely

- I am no good

Lies about Others

- He always makes dumb comments

- He is always saying things like that

- No one really likes him

- He has no respect

- He makes me miserable

- He always making me unhappy

- Why does he always do that

- He is never going to change

- He should ...

- He is no good

DEGRADING SELF

1. Self-degrading:

I am so stupid

I never get anything right.

Everything I do seem to fail. Even when I do all I can to make someone love me; they just end up rejecting me.

2. Situation Degrading:

Life is the same every day; I do not even know why I bother getting up!

Life just kicks me in the face every day—it stinks!

3. Future Degrading:

I am never going to make it in life; I do not know why I even try. It is a waste of time!

DEGRADING OTHERS

1. Degrading Others:

He is always saying rude things

He never goes a day without insulting me

Everything word out of his mouth seems to be meant for me. Even when I do all I can to make things right, he just keeps hurting my feelings.

2. Situation Degrading:

He treats me the same every day; I do not even know why I bother trying to remain friends!

He makes life miserable for me—He is not worth my efforts!

3. Future Degrading:

I am never going forgive him again; I do not know why I even try. It is a waste of time!

I will never talk with him again. Forgiveness, what is that!

I will avoid him like everyone else that mistreats me. Forgiveness? Never!

We must appreciate that our thoughts can deceive all of us, contributing to our belief that the negative mood, which has been created, because of our thinking, is reality, when it is not. If we have established a negative way of thinking, an irrational way of thinking, our mind will simply accept it as truth. Within a moment, we can alter our mood, and it is not even likely we notice it taking place. These negative feelings seem as though they are the real thing, which only reinforces to the deceptive thinking.

If we are under mental distress, and we find ourselves having anger issues or mild depression and are unhappy much of the time, we need to be in prayer for Holy Spirit. However, we need to act on behalf of our prayers as well. It is likely that we can combine our spiritual pursuits with some self-help cognitive therapy. If things have become more involved, we may want to speak with the elder or pastor. However, if we are moderately depressed, where things feel unbearable because we are having feelings of despair, we need to get some professional help from a Christian counselor. Our recommendation of a placed to find an excellent Christian counselor is found in the footnote below.[87]

Romans 15:13 Updated American Standard Version (UASV)

13 Now may the God of hope fill you with all joy and peace in believing, so that you will abound in hope by the power of the Holy Spirit.

Dr. David Burns wrote, "feelings are not facts!" Our own thinking can easily trick us. Regardless of what deception our depressed brain tells us, we will accept it as total truth. In fact, it does not take but a partial second to establish these irrational thoughts with ourselves. Therefore, in many cases, we are unlikely to notice it even happening. These negative thoughts feel so right and give credibility to the lie.

Self-Defeating Thoughts

While many are well aware that self-defeating thoughts and behavior(s) are harmful to themselves, they also know that resisting and overcoming them is another story. Self-defeating thoughts and behaviors can become deeply rooted over the years and can be extremely resistant to efforts to change them. Trying to curb such thinking can be exhausting and even painful, spiraling into depression in and of itself.

Humans being in the state of imperfection should not expect perfection in this endeavor. Our genetic heritage, inherent weaknesses, and experiences make it impossible for us to avoid all self-defeating thoughts and

---

[87] www.aacc.net/

behaviors. Therefore, lovingly, we do not demand perfection of ourselves, nor should we of others.

However, this consideration on our part does not absolve us of our responsibility to <u>control</u> our thinking and thus our feelings that lead to moods and behaviors. Behavioral scientists say that self-defeating thoughts, like good ones, are learned and developed over time. If that is correct, then self-defeating thoughts can just as surely be **un**learned! Of course, ridding ourselves of self-defeating thoughts that may have dominated our lives for years will be difficult. We should not underestimate the struggle ahead of us. There will certainly be setbacks and failures. However, rest assured, things usually get easier with time. The more we work at it, the more our new behavior will become a part of us. How?

Life: Common everyday events, both positive and negative

Thoughts: Your thinking interprets each of these events throughout the day

Mood: It is developed not by the day's events; no, it is developed by our perception of those events, by our thinking.

Every bad feeling that we have is a direct result of our bent thinking. If one finds themselves embedded in day-in-and-day-out of negative thinking, there is most certainly going to be an outburst of anger, or some mild depressive episode follow. We will not be so bold as to use the word "cause," but instead, we will say *contribute*. Thus, we will find that those continual negative thoughts will contribute to emotional spiral until it arrives at the bottom floor of a depressive episode.

Breaking Away From Bent Thinking

1. Identify and own our bent thinking. We have to self-analyze our days. We must slow down and identify what thinking error we are having and write it down. This is called mental journaling. If we are careful and wisely analyze, we can keep track of the thinking stimulus that sets off our feelings, followed by our actions. In our prayerful conversations with God, we can identify the thinking error, and internally discuss the irrational thought with God. Why is it irrational thinking? What would be the rational thought?

2. Replace the bent (irrational) thinking with rational thinking. We start self-branding ourselves: "I am no good," "I am lazy." Or we self-brand others: "he is always saying things like ..." He is rude." We should immediately stop and start to reason rationally with ourselves. "No I am not no good, this is doing nothing but making me feel worse, I am a good person who makes mistakes like everyone else." Or, "Well, he isn't always saying bad things, and we all slip in what we say at times." Positive self-talk should be done at length, keeping it honest, and aloud if possible.

3. Keep Records. Each day we need to write down the episodes of negative self-abuse, bent thinking that we go through, as well as the forms. In addition, the time spent in rationalizing with the negative thoughts. At the end of the day, summarize it in a short paragraph. We should see a decrease almost immediately in our first week.

4. Let others know. Keep our friends and family in the loop of what we are attempting to do. Periodically ask them if they notice a change in attitude and mood. Explain to them that it is best if they are honest with us. Also, prepare mentally for a possible negative feedback. Simply use the feedback as an instrument and know that more work is needed.

5. The most important key is to be practical and balanced. It took many years to achieve our way of thinking; it is not going to change overnight. In addition, if we put 50% into the putting on a new person, we will get 50% out of it. If we put 100% in, we will get 100% out of it. We should notice a small difference in a week, but we should see tremendous changes in about a four months period, some maybe six months to a year.

6. Pray to God. We need to bring God into the picture, for him, nothing is impossible.--Psalm 55:22; Luke 18:27

Read the list below of Twelve Distorted Thoughts. These were developed with the idea of focusing on the culprit that is guilty of the distortion (self), and what it is (thinking). As we work our way through this book or any self-help book, we should have the Twelve Distorted Thoughts in front of us (mentally, i.e., memorized).

Twelve Distorted Thoughts

1. SELF-ABSOLUTE (THINKING)

With this frame of mind, there is no middle ground. One who has a setback in life and sees it as nothing more than a life-ending result. To receive one bad mark on a work evaluation is the same as receiving all bad marks.

2. SELF-SWEEPING (THINKING)

If a bad event happens to us, we say: "This is the story of my life." We see our life as a never-ending series of negative events. For us, one bad event might as well be a thousand because we blow it up in our mind.

3. SELF-BRANDED (THINKING)

We own every negative event that happens in our life as being our fault. We carry the weight of the world on our shoulders. If something positive happens, it is a freak accident, because nothing good happens to us.

4. SELF-CLASSIFYING (THINKING)

As these negative events unfold on us, we own those that are not even ours; we begin to classify ourselves as "losers," "total failures," "disappointments," "let downs." It is to the point that we even begin to question why we were even born.

5. SELF-RATIONALIZING (THINKING)

We negatively perceive life, even though, much of our lives may be just fine. We refuse to acknowledge the good in our lives or the possibility of it becoming good.

6. SELF-PROPHECY (THINKING)

We see everything as ending negatively, so we end up fulfilling our own negative thinking. An adverse event happens to us, and we have already mapped out in our mind the dreadful course, followed by a tragic ending. John calls to say he **cannot** make the dinner date tonight. At once, Lisa is offering reasons as to why he has broken off the date: 'he doesn't like me;' 'he has found someone else' and on and on.

7. SELF-PSYCHIC (THINKING)

We regularly have a feeling that someone is thinking badly of us or talking badly about us without any evidence. We assume that bad things just always happen to us.

8. SELF-AMPLIFYING (THINKING)

Small negative things, events that happen to each of us every day, are amplified (to become more marked or intense) to unrealistic measures by our overactive thinking. Maybe they spill something on their shirt, are rejected from a potential date, or lose their favorite pair of shoes, so they will think, "This always happens to me!"

9. SELF-FOCUS (THINKING)

We focus in on the negative details, seeing nothing else. We refuse to see the bright side of any situation. If one attempts to point to some positive aspect of anything, we negate them and their audacity even to consider such a thing.

10. SELF-PROJECTING (THINKING)

Jim should have done this. Jane should have said this. Mark should not have done that. This is simply projecting us on everyone else.

11. SELF-LABELING (THINKING)

I am no good! I am not a good mother. I am a poor student. I am stupid.

12 SELF-PERSONALIZING (THINKING)

With no evidence, we make ourselves the scapegoat because we will always blame ourselves for everything. Lisa thinks, 'If only I were a better wife!' Lisa, as a verbally abused wife, thinks, 'it's my fault; I must be doing something wrong.' On the other hand, Lisa may scream at her husband habitually, so much so that he loses his self-esteem, "I can never do anything right.'

Dealing with Our Imperfections

Mental distress is not a part of healthy living. The important aspect is that it can be overcome by learning some simple methods that will elevate our moods. The techniques of having rational self-talk with God and identifying our irrational thinking will reduce the symptoms of a variety of mental distresses (frustration, anger, jealousy, anxiety, etc.). The idea of how we think is how we feel has been in psychology books for over one hundred years. However, it has been in God's Word, many Bible books, for about 2,000 – 3,000 years. God's Word and cognitive therapy can help us control the symptoms that lead to mental distress and help us to recreate an entirely new personality. Paul calls it putting on the new person and removing the old person.

1. Swift Improvement of Thinking Errors: For those suffering from a milder form of mental distresses such as depression or anxiety, control of thinking and the new personality can be achieved in as little as three to six months, depending on the level of effort placed into oneself.

2. The Ability to Fully Grasp: In the end, by way of deep study in God's Word, we will fully grasp exactly why our moods alter and have at our disposal, numerous principles to apply in controlling these mood swings. We will understand the difference between bent-thinking and rational thinking and be able to recognize the level of our mood.

3. Control Not Removal: Our irrational thinking is a part of the person that is imperfect; it can only be controlled, not cured. However, there will be new life-skills that we will learn to cut off and control the distorted thinking and emotion before they consume us.

4. New Person: This new person can be maintained, but we have to always be aware of the symptoms, events, and situations that can contribute to a setback.

First, one needs to recognize that ALL of their moods are brought on by our internal self-talk. This is based on the way one looks at something: perceptions, mental attitudes, and beliefs. The way we feel at this very moment is based on the self-talk that is going on between our ears.

Second, when one is distressed mentally, such as mild depressed frustration, anger, jealousy, or anxiety; really any negative mood, their thoughts are dominating the mood. We perceive not only ourselves but also the entire world in such a way that it regulates our moods. Moreover, we will buy into this false reality. If we have hit a low, we will move into the stage, believing that 'this is who I am, and it has and will always be this way.' As we reflect on the past, only those bad moments will surface. In addition, we will project this bad past as an ongoing reality for our future, creating a feeling of hopelessness.

Third, we must realize that this thinking that creates our moods are really a gross distortion of reality; this is why we are so affected by them. Although they appear valid at present, we will find that they are irrational and just downright wrong. Our mind is like a transmission in a car, where our thinking is a result of mental slippage and not an accurate perception. As we progress in rational thinking, and we begin to master methods that will help us identify this mental slippage, we will start to remove that way of thinking, and we will begin to feel better for longer periods of time until it is the norm.

Fourth, we will begin to use the Scriptures in an entirely new way. It is paramount that we take note of how the Scriptures offer us far more than the mere surface knowledge that we have grown accustomed to and see that by our having an accurate, deep understanding, with the application, we can begin to alter our old person into an entirely different person.

Bibliography

Anders, Max. *Holman New Testament Commentary: vol. 8, Galatians, Ephesians, Philippians, Colossians.* Nashville, TN: Broadman & Holman Publishers, 1999.

—. *Holman Old Testament Commentary - Proverbs .* Nashville: B&H Publishing, 2005.

Anders, Max, and Doug McIntosh. *Holman Old Testament Commentary - Deuteronomy.* Nashville: B&H Publishing, 2009.

Anders, Max, and Steven Lawson. *Holman Old Testament Commentary - Psalms: 11.* Grand Rapids: B&H Publishing, 2004.

Anders, Max, and Trent Butler. *Holman Old Testament Commentary: Isaiah.* Nashiville, TN: B&H Publishing, 2002.

Andrews, Stephen J, and Robert D Bergen. *Holman Old Testament Commentary: 1-2 Samuel.* Nashville: Broadman & Holman, 2009.

Boa, Kenneth, and William Kruidenier. *Holman New Testament Commentary: Romans.* Nashville: Broadman & Holman, 2000.

Brand, Chad, Charles Draper, and England Archie. *Holman Illustrated Bible Dictionary: Revised, Updated and Expanded.* Nashville, TN: Holman, 2003.

Butler, Trent C. *Holman New Testament Commentary: Luke.* Nashville, TN: Broadman & Holman Publishers, 2000.

Butler, Trent C. *Holman Old Testament Commentary - Hosea, Joel, Amos, Obadiah, Jonah, Micah .*

Nashville: Broadman & Holman Publishers, 2005.

Clinton, Tim, and George Ohlschlager. *Competent Christian Counseling; Volume One: Foundations and Practice of Compassionate Soul Care.* Colorado Springs, CO: WaterBrook Press, 2008.

Cooper, Rodney. *Holman New Testament Commentary: Mark.* Nashville: Broadman & Holman Publishers, 2000.

Easley, Kendell H. *Holman New Testament Commentary, vol. 12, Revelation.* (Nashville, TN: Broadman & Holman Publishers, 1998.

Gangel, Kenneth O. *Holman New Testament Commentary: Acts.* Nashville, TN: Broadman & Holman Publishers, 1998.

Gangel, Kenneth O. *Holman New Testament Commentary, vol. 4, John .* Nashville, TN: Broadman & Holman Publishers, 2000.

Garland, David E. *1 Corinthians, Baker Exegetical Commentary on the New Testament.* Grand Rapids, MI: : Baker Academic, 2003.

Harley, Willard F. Jr. *His Needs, Her Needs: Building an Affair-Proof Marriage.* Grand Rapids, MI: Revell, 2011.

Larson, Knute. *Holman New Testament Commentary, vol. 9, I & II Thessalonians, I & II Timothy, Titus, Philemon.* Nashville, TN: Broadman & Holman Publishers, 2000.

Lea, Thomas D. *Holman New Testament Commentary: Vol. 10, Hebrews, James.* Nashville, TN: Broadman & Holman Publishers, 1999.

Martin, Glen S. *Holman Old Testament Commentary: Numbers.* Nashville: Broadman & Holman Publishers, 2002.

McMinn, Mark R. *Psychology, Theology, and Spirituality in Christian Counseling (AACC Library).* Carol Stream, IL: Tyndale House Publishers, 2010.

Pratt Jr, Richard L. *Holman New Testament Commentary: I & II Corinthians, vol. 7.* Nashville: Broadman & Holman Publishers, 2000.

Walls, David, and Max Anders. *Holman New Testament Commentary: I & II Peter, I, II & III John, Jude.* Nashville: Broadman & Holman Publishers, 1996.

Weber, Stuart K. *Holman New Testament Commentary, vol. 1, Matthew.* Nashville, TN: Broadman & Holman Publishers, 2000.